THE SYRIAN CHURCH IN
MALABAR

MAVEN BOOKS

THE SYRIAN CHURCH IN
MALABAR

Joseph C. Panjikaran, B.A.

MAVEN BOOKS

Chennai   Trichy   Tirunelveli   New Delhi

MAVEN BOOKS

An Imprint of **MJP Publishers**

ISBN 978-93-87867-63-5   **MAVEN Books**

All rights reserved   No. 44, Nallathambi Street,
Printed and bound in India   Triplicane, Chennai 600 005

MJP   771   © Publishers, 2020

Publisher :   **C. Janarthanan**

Publisher's Note

The legacy of a country is in its varied cultural heritage, historical literature, developments in the field of economy and science. The top nations in the world are competing in the field of science, economy and literature. This vast legacy has to be conserved and documented so that it can be bestowed to the future generation. The knowledge of this legacy is slowly getting perished in the present generation due to lack of documentation.

Keeping this in mind, the concern with retrospective acquiring of rare books has been accented recently by the burgeoning reprint industry. MAVEN Books is gratified to retrieve the rare collections with a view to bring back those books that were landmarks in their time.

In this effort, a series of rare books would be republished under the banner, "MAVEN Books". The books in the reprint series have been carefully selected for their contemporary usefulness as well as their historical importance within the intellectual. We reconstruct the book with slight enhancements made for better presentation, without affecting the contents of the original edition.

Most of the works selected for republishing covers a huge range of subjects, from history to anthropology. We believe this reprint edition will be a service to the numerous researchers and practitioners active in this fascinating field. We allow readers to experience the wonder of peering into a scholarly work of the highest order and seminal significance.

MAVEN Books

CONTENTS

INTRODUCTION.

THE Syrian Church in Malabar is an institution which, on account of its antiquity, its wonderful preservation of the Syriac Scriptures and Liturgy, and the persecution its bishops suffered under the Portuguese, has, at all times, attracted the interest of the historian, roused the curiosity of the traveller, and elicited the wonder and admiration of the antiquarian. It is not astonishing, therefore, that several eminent writers, actuated with the best of motives, have turned their attention to the history of this interesting Church, and have produced quite a mass of literature on the subject. But, either because they had no access to reliable authorities and trustworthy documents, or because they did not fully grasp the real significance of certain events, or lastly because they had not sufficient opportunities of making local investigations and of becoming acquainted with the people and the Church they were writing about,—the fact is that even the best of these historians have made many erroneous statements. One such error seems to me to tower above all others, and is most commonly met with not merely in Magazines[1] and Reviews[2], but also in serious and learned works intended to enlighten the student of the history of this Church. This error is contained in the oft-repeated statement that the Syrian Church in the fifth century fell into the Nestorian heresy, and remained Nestorian till the Synod of Diamper in 1599, when it accepted Catholicism.

This statement I have examined in the following pages, and found to be erroneous and contrary to the facts of history. With this end in view, I have had to leave off as irrelevant to my purpose, much interesting matter specially concerning the history of the first five centuries of this Church. For the same reason I have said nothing about the famous Christian copper-plate tablets. I have divided the subject into four chapters.

---

[1] The Month, August 1912: "Christianity in the Far East."

[2] The Indian Review, July 1912: "The Syrian Church in Malabar."

In the first, I have attempted to confirm the origin of this Church from St. Thomas, because this is to some degree the basis of my thesis. In the second chapter, I have pointed out the sources from which the error originated, and have added a short sketch of the history of the Eastern Church in so far as it helps to understand the state of the Indian Church in those remote centuries. The third chapter I have devoted to a review of the Malabar Church from the origin of Nestorianism to the Synod of Diamper, with a view to show that, till the Synod, it had not succumbed to Nestorian or any other heresy. In the last chapter, I have endeavoured to show, from the very decrees of the Synod, that this Church could not at that time have been Nestorian.

THE SYRIAN CHURCH IN MALABAR.

CHAPTER I.

St. Thomas, the Apostle of India.

It is generally admitted by historians, that from very early times there existed a community of Christians on the remote shores of Southern India. The question of their origin, however, seems to have occasioned a difference of opinion. Some authors assert that this community was planted here towards the latter half of the fourth century by a Syrian merchant, Thomas of Cana; others hold that Christianity was first preached in these parts in the fifth century by Nestorian Missionaries from Persia; while a third class of writers account for the origin of these Christians by the arrival in their midst of St. Thomas, one of the Apostles of Christ.

This last view seems to be the more probable one. Eusebius, for instance, the Father of Church History, speaks of Christians in India in 190 A.D. He says that, at their request, the philospher Pantænus was sent to India by Demetrius, Bishop of Alexandria. And Pantænus bears witness to the fact that he saw with these Christians a copy of the Gospel of St. Matthew.[1] We see, therefore, that we have to fall back on the view that it was the Apostle St. Thomas who founded this Church in India. This view is also supported by the ancient tradition of the Syrian Christians themselves. Moreover, the

---

[1] Mgr. Duchesne: "The Churches separated from Rome," p. 194, London, 1907.

writings of the early Fathers and Doctors of the Church[1], such as Abdias 190 A.D., Dorotheus 254, St. Ephrem 378, St. Jerome 420, and St. Gregory of Tours 595 A.D., are in harmony with the tradition. Further, a statement in the Anglo-Saxon Chronicle, and quotations from the accounts and letters of travellers and missionaries, such as Marco Polo (1288), John of Monte Corvino (1305), Friar Odoric (1321), the Pope's legate Marignoli (1348), and St. Francis Xavier, and the works of historians, such as the learned Joseph Asseman, and the Jesuit Fathers, Peter Jarri and Maffeus,[2] give us historical information in a line with the tradition of the preaching and martyrdom of St. Thomas in India. And lastly, Epigraphy[3] by means of the recently unearthed Takt-i-Bahai inscription near Peshawar, and Numismatics by means of numerous coins found in North-West India, have afforded strong evidence of the existence of an Indo-Parthian King Gondophares to whose court St. Thomas is said in the 'Acts of Thomas' to have come.

The proofs alluded to above may be found in any book on the Apostleship of St. Thomas in India.[4] I shall not, therefore, follow the beaten track, but shall make one or two observations on points generally overlooked by historians,—I mean, the ample local evidence and the customs and manners of the people who pride themselves on having been converted by the Apostle.

Of the seven churches in Malabar said to have been founded by the Apostle, six are still standing, while the seventh, Chayal, is in ruins. Of the two families, which, as tradition testifies, were raised to ecclesiastical dignity by St. Thomas, the one, Sankoorikel (corrupted from Sankarapurikel), seems still to exist, while the other, Pakolomattam, ceased to exist only in the last century. Besides, there are still a few families which claim, as the result of a special favour promised by the Apostle, to have had priests without intermission from the time of the Apostle until the present day. Such priests call themselves the sixtieth, or the sixty-sixth from St. Thomas, according to the

---

[1] Journal of the Asiatic Society, vol. I, p. 171. London, 1885.

[2] Historia Indiæ, lib. 2. p. 31. Venice, 1589.

[3] Imperial Gazeteer of India, vol. II, pp. 5 ; 56. Oxford, 1907.

[4] Dr. Medlycott, ' India and the Apostle Thomas,' London, 1905.

order of their succession from the Great Apostle. Lately, for instance, I came across a very old manuscript history in Malayalam verse on the life and labours of St. Thomas in South India. Therein it was declared that it was the epitome of a very ancient and original work written by Maliekal Thomas, a Syrian priest who was the third in succession from St. Thomas, and that the abridgment was made by another Thomas, the father of a priest of the same family who was the forty-eighth in descent from the Apostle.

An important place-name connected with the labours of the Saint, is Chowghat. It figures in ' *Kerala Ulpathy* ' or the ' Origin of Kerala ' as Palayoor. The common tradition of Malabar associates the change of name with a miracle.[1] It is commonly believed that several Nambudhiris embraced Christianity, and if we may rely on the tradition, which, as I shall show, is supported by outstanding facts, their temple was consecrated for Christian worship. A number of Nambudhiris who refused to change their religion, left the place.[2] They cursed the land, calling it Chapakatt (சாபக்காடு), the cursed forest. The place has ever since retained the name, though it has been slightly modified into Chavakatt, and anglicised into Chowghat. This tradition concerning the name of Chowghat, and the conversion of the Nambudhiris, gains confirmation from the following facts. First, strict and orthodox Nambudhiris still consider the place as cursed, and for that reason they do not use even *pansupari* when they come there. Second, an appreciable Nambudhiri element in customs and general appearance is a noticeable feature of the Syrian Christians of those

---

[1] The miracle is this: St. Thomas found several Nambudhiri Brahmins bathing in a tank. He saw them occasionally throwing up handfuls of water. He asked them whether they could throw up the water in such a way as to cause the water-drops to stand in mid-air without falling down. They expressed their inability, and promised to follow the religion of the foreigner if he performed such a supernatural feat. St. Thomas then worked the miracle.

[2] I am informed that in the Nagara Grantha Variola of the family of the Kalathum Nambudhiri in British Malabar the following is written : ' Kali year 3153 [52 A.D.,] the foreigner Thomas Sanyasi came to our gramom, preached there, causing thereby pollution. We, therefore, came away from that gramom [Palayoor].' This, I am told, was reported by a member of that family. I did not see the original, neither could I procure a copy of it I hope some one will investigate how far this is true and whether the variola is authentic.

parts. This is corroborated by Mr. Nagam Iyah[1], who says: "There is no doubt as to the tradition that St. Thomas came to Malabar, and converted a few families of Nambudhiris. For, in consonance with this long-standing traditional belief in the minds of the people of the Apostle's mission and labours among high-caste Hindus, we have it before us to-day the fact that certain Syrian Christian women, particularly of a Desom called Kunnamkulam wear clothes as Nambudhiri women do, move about screening themselves with huge umbrellas from the gaze of profane eyes as those women do, and will not marry except perhaps in exceptional cases, and that only recently, but from among dignified families of similar aristocratic descent." And lastly, a number of Christian churches there, exhibit the peculiar architecture of Hindu pagodas. This fact was very puzzling to the Portuguese. We read in Rev. Hough[2], for instance, that Father Vincent de Lagos "was displeased at the sight of the Christian churches so closely resembling the heathen pagodas." And Rev. Whitehouse[3] says that Father de Lagos "professed disgust at the peculiar architecture of their churches, comparing them to Hindu temples, and commenced others in a style more to his European tastes."

The tradition that St. Thomas largely concerned himself with the conversion of Nambudhiris[4] and high-caste people finds further support in some of the customs that are still observed by the Syrian Christians in spite of the merciless holocaust of a great number of such customs at the Synod of Diamper. Corresponding to the 'Jatakarmam' of the Nambudhiris, the father of every Syrian Christian child, thirty six hours after its birth, mixes a little honey, ghee and gold and puts it into the mouth of the infant; six months later, the father places the child on his lap and feeds it with rice for the first time. This corresponds to the "Annaprasanam" ceremony of the Nambudhiris. Again, the barber is an indispensable person in all marriages. The "Pulakuli" ceremony is invaria

---

[1] Travancore State Manual, Vol. II, pp. 122—123. Trivandrum 1906.

[2] Christianity in India, Vol. I, p. 246. London, 1839.

[3] Lingerings of Light in a Dark Land, p. 26.

[4] Journal of the Asiatic Society, vol. I, p. 172.

bly celebrated on the tenth and eleventh day after death. This is in strict accordance with the customs of the Nambudhiris, for other sects of Hindus celebrate this ceremony on the fifteenth and sixteenth day. Meat of every kind is rigidly forbidden for this feast, and the prohibition is very strictly obeyed, and some conservative families use neither meat nor fish till the year has fully run its course, and the " Andoosrad-dham " is performed.

Let us now pass from these observations on the resemblan-ces in the customs of the Nambudhiris and the Syrian Christians, and turn our attention to some of the authorities who have written on St. Thomas, in order to see how the question stands at present. Catholic writers generally admit the Indian Aposto-late of St. Thomas. Others hold two different opinions. Basnage was the first to deny the coming of St. Thomas into India. La Croze, Tillemont and Trigaut followed him in this opinion. Among modern historians, Rev. Hough stands pre-eminent, and has made an almost classical attempt to disprove the evidence for the tradition by giving a different location to places said to be in India, and by having recourse to conjectures to explain away difficulties standing in the way of his theory. Milne Rae, Mateer, and Logan have largely drawn from the arguments of Hough without adding much original matter to his masterly exposition. Now, on the other side, foremost stands the valuable opinion of Dr. Buchanan[1] who entertained a deci-ded opinion that " we have as good authority that Apostle Thomas died in India as that Apostle Peter died at Rome." So dispassionate a scholar as Professor Wilson[2] speaks of the preaching and martyrdom of St. Thomas in India as occurren-ces very far from invalidated by any argument yet adduced against the truth of the tradition. Rev. Whitehouse[3] says that St. Thomas was the Apostle of India, and requests writers not to summarily dismiss the tradition because one or two great names doubt its truth. Dr. Kerr, Bishop Heber, and Archdeacon Robinson attribute apostolic origin to the Syrian Church of

---

[1] Christian Researches in Asia, p. 135, London, 1814.

[2] Colonel Yule's ' Marco Polo,' p. 353. Note. 4. Vol. II. London, 1903.

[3] Op. cit. p. 1.

Malabar. The simplicity and antiquity of the tradition forces Colonel Yule, the translator of Marco Polo, to support the Indian Apostolate of St. Thomas. Dr. Neale, an expert in 'eccleciastical archaeology' draws evidence from the liturgy of the Syrian Church to prove its origin from St. Thomas. Rev. D'Orsey[1], after examining all Portuguese writings, is inclined to the view that the tradition which has always prevailed in Malabar denotes a real fact.

We shall conclude these remarks with an attempt to solve two difficulties that seem to stand in the way of the Apostolic origin of the Syrian Church of Malabar, *viz.*, the meeting of the Apostle with King Gondophares and the place-name Calamina referred to as the scene of the martyrdom of the Saint.

It is now generally admitted that the Indo-Parthian king, Gondophares, who ruled over the extensive kingdoms of Afghanistan, Kandahar, Seistan, Northern and Southern Punjab, lived before 50 A.D. Professor Percy Gardner[2] says that some of the coins of Gondophares " would seem to have been struck not later than the middle of the first century," and Mr. Vincent Smith[3] admits that " all indications of his date taken together show that he must have reigned in the first half of the first century." There seems to be no reason to doubt that St. Thomas started in 35 A.D., to preach the Gospel, as Eusebius says, to the Parthians, and thence to the Medes and Persians. He visited the countries to the north-west of India, and though we must be on our guard in pinning our belief to the events chronicled in the " *Acts of Thomas*," there seems to be no difficulty in the concordance of dates, and no historical improbability in the statement that St. Thomas went to the court of the powerful king in whose territories he had preached the Gospel. He then retraced his steps, and according to Catholic tradition, which is supported by St. Gregory of Tours 590 A.D., St. John of Damascus and others, he was present at the demise of the Blessed Virgin Mary. He may then have started on his second

---

[1] Portuguese Discoveries, Dependencies, and Missions. p. 62. London, 1893.

[2] Medlycott, Op. cit, p. 7.

[3] Journal of the Royal Asiatic Society of Bengal, Jan, 1903.

Apostolic tour. He seems to have taught the Gospel in Northern Africa, Ethiopia and Arabia Felix, and taken ship at the mouth of the Persian Gulf for Socotra. From Socotra, he may have proceeded in a coasting vessel to the west coast of India, and in 52 A.D., reached Cranganore (Kodungallur), the Mouziris of older geographers, and a flourishing sea-port of those days. In this way, the apparent contradiction between the tradition of the presence of the Apostle at the court of King Gondophares, and of the scene of his labours being in South India, may be easily explained.

As to the other difficulty of the place of the martyrdom of the Apostle, historians have been at great pains to identify Calamina with the name of some town in India. They have left no map unsearched to find out Calamina, and have made many ingenious conjectures. Even Dr. Medlycott,[1] an authority on St. Thomas, makes an elaborate and very amusing attempt to derive Calamina, from " Kâlãh, the name of a place, and Elmina, which in Syriac denotes a port." To the compiler[2] of the Cochin State Manual also, Calamina has been a stumbling block. He says it cannot be identified with any town in South India, and for this reason, he pronounces the verdict of ' not proven " on the Apostolic origin of this Church.

The explanation of the difficulty seems to me to be the following. The unanimous tradition of the Syrian Christians has always pointed out the Little Mount as the scene of the Apostle's martyrdom. They called it the " Shinna Malai" (சின்ன மலை) which in English means the Little Mount. Now, just as the Portuguese in later years translated the name into "Monte Pequeno", so for the same reason, the early Syro-Chaldæan visitors and settlers called it Galmona, from the Syro-Chaldæan word, *Galma*, a rocky hill, and ' *ona* ', a diminutive suffix like the English ' ock.' Galma, and ona, Galmona thus means hillock or " Little Mount." From this the transition to Calmina, and Calamina, is easy. It seems to be in this way that the place of the Apostle's martyrdom came to be known as Calamina.

---

[1] Op. cit. pp. 150-161.
[2] Achyutha Menon, ' The Cochin State Manual,' p. 226, Cochin, 1911.

CHAPTER II.

The Early Eastern Church.

We have seen in the first chapter that the balance of opinion is on the side of the Apostolic origin of the Syrian Church of Malabar. We shall now enquire whether this Church founded by the Apostle has always followed his directions and kept the Faith taught by him, or whether, in the fifth and sixth centuries or later, it fell into the clutches of either Nestorian or any other heresy. We hope to establish that this Church followed the doctrines of the Catholic Religion till the Synod of Diamper in 1599, and that historians have made a mistake in saying that it fell into Nestorian heresy and was brought back to the Catholic Faith only in 1599 through the efforts of Archbishop Alexius Menezes of Goa.

At the very outset of this enquiry it will greatly help us to have a right understanding of the subject, if we explain how it has come about that in all the works, whether written by Protestants or Latin Catholics or Jacobite Syrian Christians, it is unanimously asserted that this Church was Nestorian till 1599. Geddes, Hough, Whitehouse, Buchanan, Milne Rae and others affirm in the clearest terms that after the first four centuries this Church fell into Nestorian heresy and was brought back under the authority of Rome by the indefatigable zeal of Archbishop Menezes. Gouvea (1606), D'Souza (1710), La Croze (1723), Joseph Asseman (1728), Le Quien, Raulin (1745), Fra Bartolomeo and several Latin missionaries have persistently maintained the same. Joseph Ittoop (1869), and a few other Jacobite writers also join in the same chorus. In short, all those who have written on this subject, are agreed in branding the Syrian Church with the stigma of Nestorian heresy.

We shall now briefly point out the origin of this error. We shall examine, for that purpose, whether all these writers are original authorities, or have derived their information from earlier writers, and if so from whom, and lastly, whether the information recorded by the early writers could be trusted.

The book that is responsible for the dissemination of this opinion throughout Europe, is the '*Jornada*'[1] of Gouvea. Antony Gouvea was a Portuguese Augustinian friar at Goa. He possessed the full confidence of Archbishop Menezes, under whose guiding hand he composed his history at the command of the Provincial of his Order in Portugal. The Archbishop was also an Austin friar. Gouvea, therefore, besides a regard for his own reputation and his obligation to obey the command of his Superior, was naturally actuated by a zeal for the credit of his Order, to give an account of the Synod favourable to the Portuguese. The Archbishop, for the same reason, took great care that nothing should be introduced tending to convey an injurious impression.[2] Gouvea had, therefore, a most difficult task. He had to obey the command of his Superior; he had to follow the advice of the Archbishop; and he had to maintain the dignity and interests of his Order. It is no wonder, then, that he failed to write an impartial account. He has given us quite a one-sided view of the subject. In 1603 he wrote in Portuguese his narrative of the tour of the Archbishop Menezes in Malabar, and his account of the Synod of Diamper. Three years later, he published it at Coimbra. It is this book that first created in the minds of the Europeans the impression that the Syrian Church was Nestorian, and that it was the unremitted labours of the Portuguese Missionaries that brought them into the pale of the Catholic Religion. Basing himself on this original work, D'Souza wrote his 'Oriente Conquistado' in 1710. La Croze, Raulin and all the succeeding writers based themselves on Gouvea. The errors of Gouvea, therefore, speedily spread all over Europe. Thenceforward the Syrian Church is considered as having been Nestorian for nearly a thousand years.

Not long after, Michael Geddes, an Edinburgh graduate who had come to Balliol College, Oxford, was sent to Lisbon in 678 as chaplain to the English factory there. During his ten years' residence abroad, he made himself thoroughly acquainted

---

[1] The full title of the book is, 'Jornata do Archbispo de Goa Sez a Serra os Christiãos de Sam Thome.'

[2] Hough, Op. cit. Vol. II, pp. 8-9.

with the Portuguese language. He obtained a copy of Gouvea, and was so captivated with the information it contained, that, when in 1688 he was forbidden by the Inquisition to continue his work as chaplain, and had to return home, he published in 1692 'The Acts and Decrees of the Synod of Diamper,' a literal English translation from the original Portuguese.[1] Two years later, basing himself on the erroneous statements contained in the *Jornada* he published in London in 1694 'The History of the Church in Malabar.'[2] This book cannot be given any more weight than a mere English re-arrangement of the work of Gouvea. This history, the first of its kind published in English, spread through all the English-speaking world the false notion that the Syrian Church had once fallen into the Nestorian heresy. With Geddes,[3] as his chief authority, Hough wrote his "Christianity in India," Whitehouse his "Lingerings of Light in a Dark Land," and Milne Rae his "Syrian Church in India.' The last writer voices the general feeling of the want of a more trustworthy and impartial guide when he says, 'It is much to be regretted that there is no history of the Synod written by a representative of the Syrian community......To foreign scholars, the Syrians likewise owe their knowledge of the history of their own Church.' The remark is very true, but we must not leave out of count the common Malabar tradition[4] as to what was actually done at the Synod of Diamper.

---

[1] G. Milne Rae, 'The Syrian Church in India.' p. VII. London 1892.

[2] Ibid, p. 193.

[3] Burnett in his 'History of the Reformation' iii. 306, says of Geddes :—"He was a learned and wise man. He had a true notion of Popery as a political combination managed by falsehood and cruelty, to establish a temporal empire in the person of the Popes. All his thoughts and studies were chiefly employed in detecting this." (Quoted in the T. S. Manual, vol. II. p. 212.) A man with such views and such an ideal before him can hardly be considered as a reliable authority.

[4] A 'padiola' document dated 20th June, 1799, written and signed at the Church of the Holy Cross, Alleppey, by the representatives of the Syrian Christian Churches, Jacobite as well as Catholic, has the following passage :— "While our ancestors were practising the Syro-Chaldæan Rite approved by the Pope, as obedient children of His Holiness, and at a time when no Syrian Catholic bishop came to govern us, Mar Alexius, Metropolitan of Goa, came to Malankara and convoked a Synod at Udiamperur." This passage shows that the Malabar tradition is that the Church was Catholic before the Synod.

Another source of this error is a confusion of terms. Nestorian is the name that is commonly applied to the Syro-Chaldaic language. When Nestorianism spread in the Eastern countries, the language of the people which was then Syro-Chadæan underwent certain modifications of character and pronunciation, and came to be known by the name of Nestorian. Nestorian and Chaldæan were therefore used as convertible terms. Consequently, historians have indiscriminately called all those who used this modified character of Estranghela or oldest Syrian, Nestorians. But it can be easily proved that, at the beginning and even at the heyday of the Nestorian heresy, there were Syro-Chaldæans in those parts, who vigorously opposed the spread of these pernicious doctrines, and defended their ancient Faith against its incursions.[1] The lives of Bishop St. Isaac of Nineveh, Bishop Sahadhuna of Urumiah, and the Monk John Saba of Dhalia, bear witness to the above statement. These lived in the sixth century and did yeoman service to the Catholic religion. Yet even these have been called Nestorians by the Western writers.[2] This practice continued for some centuries. Hence, in 1445, these Catholics, improperly called Nestorians, sent a petition to Pope Eugenius IV ; and the Pope ordered under pain of excommunication that, in future, those persons should not be called Nestorians, but Catholic Chaldæans.[3] Again, in 1553, Cardinal Maffeus, in his declaration on the state of the Chaldæan Church made before the Cardinals assembled in Rome to witness the conferring of the *pallium* on Simon Sulaka, said, " The Chaldæans seem to have had but the *name* of Nestorians, but not to have held any Nestorian error."[4] In 1580 also we find that Mar Elia, Archbishop of Amed, in a letter to Cardinal Carafa at Rome, begged His Eminence to obtain an order from the Holy See to abolish the improper practice of addressing the Syro-Chaldæans as

---

[1] George E. Khayyath, " Syri Orientales, seu Chaldœi Nestoriani et Romanorum Pontificum Primatus," Rome, 1870.

[2] Joseph Asseman, " Bibliotheca Orientalis," t. I, p. 444 ; t. IV. p. 41 et seq., Rome, 1728.

[3] Samuel Giamil, " Genuinœ Relationes inter Sedem Apostolicam et Assyriorum Orientalium seu Chaldœorum Ecclesiam." p. 11., Rome, 1902.

[4] Ibid. Appendix I. Document III. p. 480.

Nestorians, and to call them Oriental Chaldæans or Assyrian Catholics.[1] Thus we see that it was very common to call the Chaldæan Catholics, Nestorians, and it is not strange, therefore, that historians in India[2] considered them all heretics.

We shall now briefly examine the history of the Eastern Church, specially in the fifth and sixth centuries, in order to see whether and how far the course of events that affected the history of this Church, produced corresponding results in the Indian Church which was united to it even from early times.

Towards the close of the second century, Ahad Abuei[3], who had been elected Bishop of Seleucia, went to Antioch to be consecrated. But he was attacked by the Persians, at the instigation of their king. He managed to escape to Jerusalem, but his companion Kam-Jesus fell into their hands, and was put to death. On hearing this disastrous news, the Patriarch of Antioch allowed the bishop to be consecrated in Jerusalem, and declared that in future bishops chosen for the see of Seleucia, might be consecrated in Seleucia itself, and that they need not go to Antioch for consecration.[4] Soon after this concession, the Primate of Persia was consecrated Metropolitan of Great India. Both these facts are attested by the Council of Nice in 325. The former custom is recorded by the 33rd Canon of the Council. "Let the See of Seleucia which is one of the Eastern cities be honoured likewise and have the title of Catholicon, and let the prelate thereof ordain Archbishops, as the other Patriarchs do, that so the Eastern Christians who live under heathens may not be wronged by awaiting the Patriarch of Antioch's leisure, or by going to him, but may have a way opened to them to supply their own necessities; neither will any injury

---

[1] Ibid. Doc. xxv. pp. 90-97.

[2] "These Christians are indiscriminately called St. Thomas Christians, Nestorians, Syrians, and sometimes the Malabar Christians of the mountains, by the Portuguese writers of that time and by the subsequent missionaries from Rome." Asiatic Researches, vol. VII, p. 362. 'Account of the St. Thomas Christians on the coast of Malabar' by F. Wrede Esq. Mr. Mackenzie in the ' Travancore State Manual,' vol. II. p. 157, has the following :—" It must be conceded that the epithet Nestorian is loosely used by the Portuguese writers, and sometimes denotes a member of the Oriental Church without connoting any idea of heresy."

[3] Joseph Guriel, " Elementa Linguae Chaldaicæ, et Series Patriarcharum Chaldæorum " p. 152. Rome, 1860.

[4] Samuel Giamil, Op. cit. p. 542.

be done to the Patriarch of Antioch thereby, seeing that he has consented to its being thus, upon the Synod's having desired it of him."[1] The latter custom is to be inferred from the signature of one of the prelates present at the Council. The prelate signs himself as "John the Persian [presiding over] the Churches in the whole of Persia and Great India." We have no proofs that Bishop John was the actual reigning prelate of Great India, and it is very improbable that a bishop could exercise direct and immediate jurisdiction over two such distant bishoprics as Persia and India. The signature of the bishop also merely implies the ultimate control he held over the Indian Church. We see, therefore, that, at the Council of Nice, Seleucia was withdrawn from the jurisdiction of Antioch, and was erected into an independent Catholicon or Patriarchate. The Patriarch was given power to consecrate Bishops and Archbishops for the Eastern Christians. Persia, therefore, came under his authority, and as it was the Primate or Metropolitan of Persia that consecrated bishops for the Indian Church, this Church was also brought indirectly under the control of Seleucia.

Let us now turn to the origin and progress of Nestorianism. In 428 A.D., Nestorius, a monk of the Monastery of Eprepius, was chosen by the Emperor Theodosius II to be the Patriarch of Constantinople in succession to Sissinius. Consecrated in April of the same year, he showed great zeal against the few remaining advocates of the Arian heresy. But while combating one heresy, he fell into another. He had allowed Anastasius, a newly ordained priest of Constantinople, to preach against the heretics. In one of his sermons, Anastasius said that it was improper to give Mary the title " *Theotokos* " or Mother of God. " Let no one," said he, " designate the Blessed Virgin as the Mother of God. Mary was merely human and God cannot be born of a human creature."[2] Nestorius, instead of contradicting this declaration, advocated the view advanced by Anastasius.

---

[1] Hough, Vol. I. p. 245.

[2] John Alzog, " Universal Church History," vol. I. p. 415, Dublin 1895.

According to the view of Nestorius, the Incarnation was merely "the indwelling of God the Word in the man Jesus, and consequently God had not been truly made man." In its further development it necessarily led to the conclusion that there were two sonships, one Divine, and the other human, one of God and the other of the Virgin Mary; and that there were two persons, entirely distinct and separate, between whom there existed only an external or moral and not a hypostatic union.[1]

Cyril, Patriarch of Alexandria, was the great opponent of Nestorius. To discuss these new doctrines, the Emperor Theodosius II convoked the Council of Ephesus in 431. There were 256 bishops present. They examined the writings of Nestorius, discussed the term 'Theotokos', and finally the Council unanimously condemned the doctrines of Nestorius.

The writings of Nestorius, however, found favour with some influential persons, and two of them, Ibas and Thomas Barsumas, were obliged to leave the school of Edessa for their advocacy of the Nestorian heresy. To none of all its friends is the Nestorian Faith indebted so much as to Barsumas, who was created bishop of Nisibis in 435.[2] The Nestorians, who had been turned out of their homes at Edessa, were protected by him. In 498 Babæus, whom Barsumas had won over to Nestorianism, ascended the throne of Seleucia. The following year, he held a synod in which the Nestorian party was organised. The Catholicon of Seleucia thus became Nestorian.

It must not be imagined, however, that all the bishops, priests and people followed the Patriarch in this change of religion. There were Catholics in all the countries under the authority of Seleucia. Le Quien[3] says:—Although the Nestorian heresy had spread itself in all the regions of the Persian Empire, yet there were not wanting in those places, persons who preserved the Catholic Faith free from both Nestorian and

<hr>

[1] John Alzog, op. cit. p. 416.

[2] Lawrence Von Mosheim, "Institutes of Eccleciastical History" Vol. I. pp 475-476; 478. London 1895.

[3] Oriens Christianus, tom. II. coll. 1086, Paris 1240.

and Jacobite[1] heresies and they were called by those two sects Melkites. Joseph Asseman[2] asserts that in 528 the greater part of the Christians of Persia were Catholics. Not only were there Catholics in those places, but we have also some proofs of the existence of a line of Catholic Metropolitans in Seleucia, under the authority of the Melkite Patriarch of Antioch. Le Quien,[3] for instance, quotes the testimony of Barhebræus and other eminent writers to show that the Nestorian Patriarch Abraham had obtained from the Sultan an order that the Primate of the Melkites or orthodox Chaldæans should not be called Catholicos and should not consecrate bishops for the provinces under him. The Catholicus of the Melkites, on account of this noxious order of the Sultan, had to consecrate Bishops and Archbishops for the provinces under him, in secret and during night. When in 911 A.D., the Melkite Catholicus was consecrating a bishop, the Nestorian Patriarch came to know of it by means of his spies and had them both taken before the Sultan who imposed heavy fines on them. It is through these Chaldæan Catholici that the Catholic Patriarchs of Antioch claimed Asia, India etc., as part of their Patriarchate, and not because they ever sent bishops, or directly governed those provinces.[4] In 1050, the Catholic Patriarch of Antioch wrote that his see was large and extensive and that he had under him two

---

[1] This heresy takes its name from Jacob Baradæus or Zanzalus, who vigorously advocated the Eutychian or Monophysite doctrine on the nature of Christ. The essence of this doctrine is that, when Christ took the human nature, His flesh, by its union with the Godhead, had been mingled and blended with the Divine nature and absorbed by it. Consequently, the body of Christ was not in substance a human body, but merely appeared to be so to the external senses. It was, therefore, the Deity who immediately suffered and was crucified.

It is unnecessary for us to enter into the question whether the Indian Church was Jacobite. For no historian of any standing has answered this question in the affirmative. Moreover, even the recent efforts of certain Jacobites have not, it seems to me, brought forward any valid arguments which demand an answer. The only mention of a Jacobite bishop in these parts is made by Francis Day *Land of the Perumals*. p. 216) who says that in 696 a Jacobite bishop came to Malabar. But he does not tell us on what authority he bases this statement. All historians, however, including Mr. Day, are agreed that the Jacobite Patriarch did not exercise any jurisdiction over the Indian Church before 1663. We see, therefore, that the Indian Church before the Synod of Diamper must have been either Nestorian or Catholic.

[2] Op. cit. tom. 4. p. 91.

[3] Op. cit. coll. 1086-1087.

[4] Travancore State Manual, Vol. II, p. 202.

Catholici, to whom were subject Asia, India, and other countries.[1]
This is probably all the evidence we have of the existence of a
line of Catholic Metropolitans, or Catholici.

Let us now turn to the events that affected the Church in
Persia. The Persian Church had been founded by missionaries
from Syria[2], and its language, discipline and doctrines were, therefore, identical with those of the Syrian Church. From the beginning of the fourth century, it was governed by numerous
bishops, and a little later, this episcopate was divided into
eccleciastical provinces governed by Metropolitans. "*The
Metropolitan of Persia had suffragans* on both sides of the
Persian Gulf and even beyond it in the islands of Socotra,
Ceylon, and *on the Coasts of Malabar*."[3]

During this time and for some centuries following, the
Persian Church suffered severe persecutions. The persecuted
Christians and even Bishops, at least on two occasions, sought an
asylum in Malabar. Sapor II (310-381) began a cruel persecution of the Christians. A colony of 400 Christians, therefore
left their native land, and in 345 betook themselves to the
hospitable shores of Malankara, where, along with the native
Christians, they were permitted to freely practise their
religion. In the fifth century, as we have seen, the peace of
the Persian Church was disturbed by theological disputes.
About 500 A.D., the arms of Nushirvan and his fiercer grandson
were assisted by Nestorian sectaries who still lurked in the
native cities of the East, and their zeal was rewarded by the
gift of Catholic churches, which were, however, soon after
recovered by the Emperor Heraclius.[4] In his treaty with the
Persian king Chosroes I, the Emperor Justinian (518 A.D - 56?
A.D.) introduced some conditions which tended to the toleration
of Catholicism in Persia.[5] In the long contest that raged

---

[1] Paulinus Bartolomeo, "India Orientalis Christiania" p. 94, Rome, 1794

[2] "It is certain from Eusebius (Eccl. History, Bk. III, ch. 23) that the Christian Faith was planted in Persia as early as the Apostolic Church." (Sozomen
Eccl. History, Bk. II, ch. 9, p. 63, note 3, London ; 1860).

[3] Mgr. L. Duchesne. Op. cit. p. 15. The Italics within all the quotations in
these pages are ours.

[4] Gibbon, 'Decline and Fall of the Roman Empire,' vol. V, p. 178, Lon. 1898

[5] Ibid, vol V, p. 39.

between Rome and Persia, the Catholics generally suffered persecution[1] as being in sympathy with the Romans who professed the same religion. The *rôle* of the Persian Kings as persecutors of Christians was now played by the Caliphs. In 682 they conquered Persia, captured Antioch in 698, and for more than two centuries, the persecution lasted with only brief intervals. One consequence was that a second colony of oppressed Christians with two Bishops started for Malabar and reached Quilon in 880 A.D.

We have seen that, when in 498[2] the Catholicus of Seleucia became Nestorian, some of the bishops, priests and people refused to acknowledge him any longer as their religious head, and held fast to the ancient Faith. One of the most important of these bishops was the ·Primate of Persia. It is very necessary to investigate this point, for we have seen that the Indian Church was linked to the Persian and was supplied with bishops by the Primate of Persia. We have, however, an important document which supports our statement. It is a letter which has been overlooked by several historians, and has not been given the importance it deserves by others who have noticed it.

Jesujabus Adjabenus or Jesuab of Adiabene, who was the Nestorian Patriarch of Seleucia from 650 - 660, in his letter[3] No. 14, to Simon, the Primate of Persia and Metropolitan of Ravardshir,[4] says :—

"Since the gift of God has been flowing through the narrow ways of the canons, and through lawful messengers,

---

[1] Dr. Giesseler, vol. II, p. 20, Edinburgh.

[2] Dr. Neander (vol. IV. p. 73) gives 496 A.D. But Prof. Kurtz, quoted by Rae (p. 107), has 498 A.D. The latter date seems to be more exact, since the Council of Seleucia, which was assembled soon after the accession of Babæus, is admitted by all to have taken place in 499 A.D.

[3] Joseph Asseman. Op. cit., tom III., pp. 113-ff.

" Quum per legitimos traductores, perque canonum semitas donum Dei fluxerit fluatque ; en plenus est orbis terrarum episcopis, sacerdotibus et fidelibus, qui tanquam stellae caeli de die in diem augentur. At in vestra regione, ex quo ab eccleciasticis canonibus deficistis, interrupta est ab Indiae populis sacerdotalis successio ; nec India solum—quae a maritimis regni Persarum usque ad Colon, spatii ducentorum super mille parasangarum extenditur—sed et ipsa Persarum regio vestra, divina doctrinæ lumine, quod per Episcopis veritatis refulget, orbata et in tenebris jacet."

[4] Ibid, p. 127.

allow it to flow. Behold, the earth is full of bishops, priests and faithful, who, like the stars of heaven, are increasing every day. But in your country, from the time you have revolted from the canons of the Church, the succession of priesthood has been cut off from the people of India; *nor from India alone,* which extends from the shores of Persia as far as Colon (Quilon)—a space of more than twelve hundred parasangs.[1]—*but also your own country of Persia lies in darkness deprived of the light of Divine doctrine which shines forth through bishops of the Truth.*"

Francis Day[2] seems to have this letter in mind when he says that the Nestorian Patriarch declared "that the Churches in Persia and India were in a declining state owing to the neglect of the Primate of Persia stating that *as he now refused to acknowledge the authority of Seleucia, the succession of priesthood had been cut off from India. Relying upon Apostolic succession direct from St. Thomas, the Primate of Persia now considered the authority of the Patriarch of Seleucia unnecessary.*" Whitehouse,[3] noticing this letter, merely says that the Persian Metropolitan revolted against the Patriarch of Seleucia for some " unexplained cause." Dr. Medlycott[4] and Mr. Mackenzie[5] merely mention the revolt without drawing any inference whatever from it.

This letter clearly shows that when the Catholicos of Seleucia became Nestorian, the Primate of Persia, true to his religion, refused any longer to obey a head who had strayed away from the ancient Faith. And the Nestorian Patriarch did not succeed in winning over the Persian Metropolitan, before the ninth century. Till that time, the Metropolitan, seeing that he had no immediate Catholic superior, ' relied,' as Day says, ' on Apostolic succession direct from St. Thomas,' and continued independent of Seleucia for a century and a half, when we have the first recorded instance of these facts. Day is not quite exact when he says that the Metropolitan considered the supe- rior authority ' unnecessary '. It is more correct to say that he

---

[1] A parasang is nearly equivalent to $3\frac{1}{4}$ miles.   [2] Op. cit. p. 125.

[3] Op. cit. p. 43.   [4] Op. cit. p. 155.   [5] Christianity in Travancore, p. 5.

found it indefensible and opposed to his obligations as a Catholic prelate. And the 'unexplained cause,' alluded to by Mr. Whitehouse, is to be explained by the refusal of the Metropolitan to follow his superior in the change of religion. During all this time, then, the Indian Church remained Catholic through the Catholic Metropolitans of Persia.

The Metropolitans of Persia continued independent of Seleucia till the time of the Nestorian Patriarch Timotheus[1] who resided at Bagdad. But in 800 A D. the Metropolitan submitted to the Patriarch, and Persia thus became Nestorian.

But at that time and long after, there have been faithful Catholic bishops, priests and people in Persia, Syria, Mesopotamia, and all the countries affected either by Nestorian or Jacobite heresy, in which the jurisdiction was directly exercised by the Patriarch of Seleucia or indirectly by the Metropolitan of Persia.[2] Moreover several Nestorian and Jacobite bishops abjured their doctrines and joined the Catholic Church.

In 945, for instance, several Nestorian bishops of Cappadocia, Media, Persia and both Armenias, joined the Church of Rome.[3] In 1145 there was a union of the Nestorians of Armenia with the Catholic Church.[4] Mar Timothy, Chaldæan Archbishop of Cyprus-Tarsis, was received in communion by Pope Eugene IV at the Florentine Council.[5] There were other illustrious persons in those parts who followed the Catholic Religion. Their names can be found in the ponderous volumes of Joseph Asseman, who is very exhaustive and is, on the whole, a reliable authority on the history of the Eastern Church.

---

[1] "Nestorianorum Catholicon seu Patriarcha Timotheus (778 - 820) qui residebat Bagdadi." Wouters, 'Compendium Historiæ Ecclesiasticæ', p. 256.

[2] Surveying the history of the Eastern Church from the 5th to the 9th centuries, Fortescue remarks :—" A very large number of Christians have left the union of the Catholic Church, yet we find established throughout the Empire one great corporate body, far greater than all the schismatical churches put together, which, in spite of such nicknames as Melkite, Dyophysite, and so on, is always officially known as the Orthodox Catholic Church. Throughout this Catholic Church, the Pope reigns as overlord and chief; it is divided into the five patriarchates and the autocephalous Church of Cyprus." Adrian Fortescue, ' The Orthodox Eastern Church,' p. 71, London, 1908.

[3] Asseman. Op. cit. t. 4. p. 407.

[4] Ibid. tom. 4, p. 94.

[5] Werner, ' Orbis Catholicus ', p. 166, Friborgh, 1890.

Let us close this chapter with an examination of the statement that is commonly made even by historians of high standing, that there have been no Catholic Patriarchs of Seleucia from
the time of Babæus to that of Simon Sulaka (1553). Yet a close
study of the pages of Asseman, Le Quien, Guriel and others, and
a careful perusal of the Vatican documents which have been recently searched out by the learned Samuel Giamil, Procurator-
General of the Catholic Chaldæan Patriarch at the court of Rome
and published in 1902 under the title, " Genuine Relations between the Apostolic See and the Chaldæan Patriarchs," reveals
the undeniable fact that, so early as the 8th century forward,
there have been Catholic Patriarchs on the throne of Seleucia.

Joseph Guriel, who has composed a " Catalogue of Chal-
dæan Patriarchs," says, " Historians assert that Marimme, who
sat on the throne of Seleucia for four years (758-762), abjured
Nestorianism and joined the Roman communion during the
Pontificate of Stephen III." [1]   In 1226, Mar Sabar Jesu V, the
Patriarch of the Chaldæans, sent his profession of faith to Rome
through his vicar Ara. It was also signed by the Archbishop of Nisbis, two other Archbishops, and three Bishops.
This interesting document may be read in Giamil. [2] In 1247,
Mar Makika II requested communion with Rome and sent his
profession of fa'th through his legate Andreas to Pope Innocent
IV. [3]   In 1304, Mar Jabalaha III (1281-1317) sent a letter to
Pope Benedict XI, containing his profession of faith and request-
ing reconciliation with the Catholic Church. [4]   From 1490-1599,
we shall show elsewhere that all the Patriarchs of Seleucia were
Catholics. Suffice it to note here, that, at the confirmation of
Sulaka as Patriarch of Seleucia in 1553, the Pope Julius III
declared that the discipline and liturgy of the Syrians had al-
ready been approved by his predecessors Nicolas I (858-867)
Leo X (1513-1521), and Clement VII (1523-1534) [5]

---

[1] Joseph Guriel. Op. cit. p. 168.

[2] Op. cit. pp. 1-4.

[3] Joseph Guriel. p. 188.

[4] Samuel Giamil. pp. 5-8.

[5] Mackenzie. " Christianity in Travancore," p. 92, Trivandrum, 1901.

CHAPTER III.

The Indian Church from 498 A.D. - 1599 A.D.

In this chapter we shall investigate the state of the Indian Church from the close of the fifth century to the beginning of the seventeenth, and we shall pay special attention to the religion of the bishops who have governed this Church.

The first historical notice of the Indian Church after a Nestorian Catholicos had occupied the see of Seleucia, is given by Cosmas Indicopleustes who visited India in 522 A.D. In his "Christian Topography"[1] he says :—"We have found the Church not destroyed but very widely diffused and the whole world filled with the doctrine of Christ which is being day by day propagated and the Gospel preached over the whole earth. This, as I have seen with my own eyes in many places, I, as a witness of the truth, relate. In the island of Taprobane to the interior India (*ad interiorem Indiam*) where the Indian Ocean is, there exists a Christian Church where clergy (*clerici*) and faithful are found. So also in Male, as they call it, where the pepper grows. But at Kalliana (they call it thus) there is a bishop generally ordained in Persia; similarly also, in the island which is called Diascoris, situated in the Indian sea, priests are found who have been ordained in Persia and sent thither."

We must remember that at this time Justinian was the Roman Emperor, and that during his reign, to use the words of Gibbon, "it became difficult to find a church of the Nestorians within the limits of the Roman Empire," and the Nestorians had all been crushed by the penal laws.[2] Moreover we have seen that during this time and the three centuries following, Persia was Catholic. Hence, bishops ordained in Persia who came to the Indian Church, could not have been Nestorians. Further, from the words of Cosmas, "we have found the Church not destroyed, but very widely diffused," we may infer that he is speaking of the ancient Faith which, there was a tradition, had

---

[1] Bibliotheca veterum patrum, t. 2. liber III. pp. 449-450, quoted in Giamil, p. 615.

[2] Gibbon. Op. cit. vol. V, p. 146.

been long established in India. This, it seems to me, is what he means, for he writes to his brethren at home that the rumour that the ancient Church was destroyed is not true, and that he has seen this Church with his own eyes not destroyed but widely diffused. Nestorianism, moreover, had been seated on the throne of Seleucia only for twenty-four years. We cannot believe that within so short a period it could have been established in India and also destroyed. In any case, therefore, the bishop whom Cosmas met in India could not have been a Nestorian, and there is nothing in the words of Cosmas to show that he was one. I am, therefore, at a loss to understand how writers, basing themselves on this passage from Cosmas, maintain that the Malabar Church at this time was Nestorian.

In a previous section, we have made it clear that the Indian Church was dependent on Persia and that it was the Metropolitan of Persia who consecrated bishops for this Church. We have also shown that when the Catholicos of Seleucia became Nestorian in 498 A.D., the Metropolitan of Persia refused to obey him and continued in that state of independence till the time of the Nestorian Patriarch Titmotheus in 800 A.D. All this time the Indian Church practised the Catholic religion and was obedient to the Catholic Metropolitans of Persia. But what was the condition of the Indian Church after 800 A.D.? The common answer to this question is that till the beginning of the 17th century this Church was Nestorian. We have, however strong grounds to doubt the validity and accuracy of this answer.

After 800 A.D., it would appear that the Indian Church broke off its communion with the Metropolitan of Persia who had now become Nestorian, and indeed with the Eastern Church altogether till 1490. There seems to be only one instance of intercourse during this time between this Church and the Persian. It was in 880 A.D., when, as we have seen, two bishops came to Quilon as a result of persecutions at home. But after this event, for a period of more than seven centuries, we have no authentic record of the coming here of any bishop from the Eastern Church. There seems to be a haze over this period of the history of the Indian Church, for the records for the history of this period are very meagre. But, in what we possess, we find no mention made of any bishop coming to India from the East before 1490. Consequently, to understand the real state of the Indian Church during these " dark ages," we have to turn to the letters and writings of Missionaries who have come to India from the beginning of the 14th century onward, and we must understand correctly the significance of the inscription on the two crosses which have fortunately been preserved to this day.

Let us then examine the evidence afforded by the bas-relief crosses with Pahlavi inscriptions, which are to be seen in the churches at the St. Thomas Mount and at Kottayam. Dr. Burnell[1] is of opinion that the earliest settlements in South India were Persian and that a few inscriptions still remain which belong to that period. The most famous of these inscriptions, he says, is the miracle-working cross of St. Thomas at the Mount near Madras. There are two crosses of a similar make which may be seen in the Syrian Church at Kottayam. Of these two crosses the earlier appears to be the one in the south wall of the Kottayam Old Church. Judging from the formation of the letters Dr. Burnell[2] places this cross and the one at the Mount not later than the 7th or 8th century. The other cross behind a side altar of the same church, is dated at least two centuries later. Besides a line in Pahlavi, it contains also one in the ordinary Estranghela character.

Scholars have given various readings, and consequently various translations, of the inscriptions around the cross. The inscription on the cross at the Mount and on the older cross at Kottayam has been thus rendered by Dr. Burnell[3] : — " In punishment by the cross was the suffering of this one, who is the true Christ, God above and Guide ever pure." Dr. Haug translates it thus :—" He that believes in the Messiah and in God in the height and also in the Holy Ghost is in the grace of Him who suffered the pain of the Cross." Dr. West gives

---

1 Burnell's South Indian Palography, p. 57, London, 1878.

2 Indian Antiquary, vol. III, p. 311.

3 Ibid. pp. 311-316.

a still different rendering — What freed the true Messiah, the forgiving, the upbraiding from hardship ? The crucifixion from the tree and the anguish of this."

The translation given by Dr. Burnell is generally admitted to be the best. It is clear from it that the One who suffered punishment by the cross ' *is the true Christ and God above,*' *i. e.*, He had the true human nature and the Divine, and was, therefore, at the time of the crucifixion, both man and God. Now, this belief, as we have seen, is opposed to Nestorianism, which inculcates that only the man Christ suffered. Consequently these bas-relief crosses declare one of the doctrines of the Catholic Church, and they must have been planted here as monuments of the Catholic Religion by some Persian Catholic missionaries. This conclusion is confirmed by the fact that the Metropolitan of Persia was Catholic at the date attributed to the crosses by Dr. Burnell.

The inscription on the later cross at Kottayam has been thus rendered by Dr. Burnell[1] : Estranghela Syriac — Let me not glory except in the cross of our Lord Jesus Christ." Pahlavi —" Who is the true Messiah and God above and Holy Ghost."

Even taking this translation[2] as it stands, it is opposed to the doctrines of Nestorianism. For it says that Our Lord Jesus Christ " who is the true Messiah and *God above,* and Holy Ghost, suffered on the cross, *i.e.*, the Godhead suffered on the cross. Hence it is clearthat this bas-relief cross and this inscription could not have been put up here by Nestorians.

---

[1] Indian Antiquary, vol. III, p. 314.

[2] I think that this translation of Dr. Burnell is inexact, for it may mean that Jesus Christ, who is the true Messiah, or the Second Person of the Trinity, God above, or God the Father, and the Holy Ghost or the Third Person of the Trinity, *i.e.*, the whole Trinity suffered on the cross. This form of belief has not been held by any Christian body in Persia, Syria or Malabar. The translation of Dr. Haug is therefore preferable. " Who believes in the Messiah and God above and in the Holy Ghost, is redeemed through the grace of Him who bore the cross." Here it is stated that every one who believes in the Trinity, is redeemed through the grace of the Second Person of the Trinity who bore the cross—a doctrine opposed to Nestorianism but accepted by the Catholic Church.

The following general remark by Dr. Burnell strongly supports, not merely the particular view I have drawn from the inscription on the crosses, but my thesis as a whole. He says :[1]—" The Syrians (Nestorians and Jacobites) appear to have had very little influence over the Christians in the West Coast of Southern India, before the 16th century; for the early Catholic Missionaries speak generally of Christians of St. Thomas[2] and not of Nestorian heretics."

The next event in the history of the Indian Church is the arrival in 880 A.D. of two bishops, Mar Sapor and Mar Prodh. Le Quien[3] says that " these bishops were Chaldæans and had come to Quilon soon after its foundation. They were men illustrious for their sanctity, and their memory was held sacred in the Malabar Church. They constructed many churches and, during their lifetime, the Christian religion flourished especially in the kingdom of Diamper." They led so saintly a life that many churches were dedicated in their name, and we shall see that Archbishop Menezes changed the names of such churches, and dedicated them to " All Saints " at the Synod of Diamper, for the mere reason that they came from Babylon. There is, moreover, not a shred of evidence to prove that they were Nestorians.[4]

In the year 1122, we come across a valuable piece of information to which, in my opinion, sufficient importance has not been given by historians. We read in the life of Pope Calixtus II,[5] in the chronicle of Albericus written in the 13th century, in Le Quien[6] and others, that Archbishop Mar John of India, otherwise known as Patriarch of India, went with his Suffragan Bishops to Constantinople. There, at the court of

---

[1] Indian Antiquary, vol. III, p. 311, footnote.

[2] " The nation in general are called the St. Thomas Christians. This is their name in all parts of India, and it imports an antiquity that reaches far beyond the Eutychians or Nestorians or any other sect." Claudius Buchanan, 'Christian Researches in Asia,' p. 126, London, 1814.

[3] Op. cit. t. 2. coll. 1275.

[4] Giamil. Op. cit. pp. 582-584.

[5] Rev. Horace K. Mann, " The Lives of the Popes in the Middle Ages," pp. 216-220, vol. VIII, London, 1910.

[6] Op. cit. t. 2. coll. 1276-1277.

John II Comnenus, he found the envoys whom Calixtus II had sent to promote the union of the Greek and Roman Churches. The Archbishop went with them to Rome, received the *pallium*, and exposed before the Pope and the Cardinals the miracles that were wrought at the tomb of St. Thomas in Mylapore. These facts are well authenticated, and cannot be denied. If the Indian Church was at this time Nestorian, the Archbishop should have gone to the Catholicos of Seleucia, or to the Metropolitan of Persia, his immediate superior. The very fact that the Archbishop went to Constantinople and to distant Rome, points to the fact that he professed the Catholic Religion, and consequently, the Indian Church of which he was Archbishop or Patriarch, was also Catholic.

Let us now consider the writings of some missionaries and travellers which throw light on the condition of the Indian Church. John of Monte Corvino was the first Latin missionary to visit India. On his way to China in 1291 he landed in India. In the two letters he wrote from China in 1305 and 1306, he says not a word on the Nestorianism of the Christians, but merely mentions that " the people persecute much the Christians and all who bear the Christian name."

In 1328, Pope John XXII, who was residing at Avignon, consecrated Jordanus, a Dominican friar, as bishop of Quilon.[1] He was sent in 1330 with a letter addressed to the chief of the Nazaranes in Quilon. If at that time the Christians of Quilon were Nestorians or any other congregation except Catholics, the Pope would not have sent a bishop to them, for we cannot imagine a bishop without a diocese which he has to administer and without people whom he has to govern. We conclude therefore, that the people to whom the Pope sent Bishop Jordanus were Catholics.

A valuable evidence of the true condition of the Indian Church is forthcoming in the year 1348. In that year Pope Clement VI sent the Franciscan Bishop, John de Marignoli, as his legate to these Christians. Marignoli says[2] :—" Nor are

---

[1] Milne Rae. Op. cit. p. 193.
[2] Travancore State Manual, vol. II, p. 145.

the Saracens the proprietors of pepper, but the Christians of St. Thomas. And these latter are the masters of the public weighing office, from which *I derived as a perquisite of my office as Pope's legate*, every month, a hundred gold fanams and a thousand when I left...... So, after a year and four months, I took leave of the brethren."

Finding themselves powerful, the Christians chose a king from among themselves, to rule over them.[1] The orthodoxy of this dynasty is clear from the testimony of Pope Eugene IV, who, in 1439, sent to the reigning prince the following letter[2] :—" To my most beloved son in Christ, Thomas, the illustrious Emperor of the Indians, Health and Apostolic Benediction. There has often reached us a constant rumour that *your Serenity and all who are the subjects of your kingdom are true Christians.*"

These two passages clearly prove that the Indian Church at this time was Catholic. In the first instance, it is absurd to believe that the Pope would send his legate to a Nestorian people, and that they would gladly receive him, and pay him monthly, as a perquisite of his office, 100 gold fanams, and ten times that sum when he left. In the second, the Pope styles the Emperor his most beloved son in Christ, and bears witness to the constant rumour he has heard that the Emperor and all the subjects of his kingdom are true Christians.

The next historical mention of this Christian community is to be found in the "Travels of Ludovico di Varthema."[3] Varthema says in 1505 :—" In this city (Kayenkolam or Quilon) we found some *Christians of those of St. Thomas,* some of whom are merchants and *believe in Christ as we do.* They say that every three years a priest comes there to baptise them, and that he comes there from Babylon. These Christians keep Lent longer than we do, but they keep Easter like ourselves, and they all observe the same solemnities that we do. But they say Mass like the Greeks." It is evident from this that the belief in the incarnation of Christ that obtained in the Indian

---

[1] Journal of the Asiatic Society, vol. I, p. 179,   London, 1885.
[2] Travancore State Manual, vol. II, p. 147.
[3] Translated by Winter Jones, p. 180,   Haklyut Society,   London, 1863.

Church was the same as that of the Catholic Church to which di Varthema belonged. Moreover, it is apparent that this Church observed Lent and Easter, but they said Mass in the Syriac Rite. We are informed also that the Syrian Church was dependent on Babylon at this time. But the see of Babylon, as we shall show, was governed by a Catholic prelate. We have, therefore, to conclude that the Indian Church was Catholic.

Mr. Mackenzie, in his article on 'Christianity in Travancore,'[1] after discussing the contention that ' the St. Thomas Christians before the arrival of the Portuguese were not Nestorian heretics,' merely admits that it is 'a possible view which can be argued.' His most important argument for not giving his fullest support to the contention is ' the historical fact that they obtained five bishops from the Patriarch of Babylon, and that the Patriarchs of Babylon were Nestorians.'

Mar Simon, Patriarch of the East, at the request of the Indian Christians, sent them in 1490 two bishops, Mar Thomas and Mar John. Mar Thomas after a time returned to the Patriarch, leaving Mar John alone to administer the Indian Church. On the death of Mar Simon in 1502, Mar Elias, his successor consecrated three monks from the monastery of St. Eugene under the names of Mar Jaballa, Mar Denha and Mar Jacob. These started for India in company with Mar Thomas, and found the aged Mar John still living. These are the bishops alluded to by Mr. Mackenzie.

In 1504, these bishops sent a long report to their Patriarch. The full report may be read in Giamil.[2] We take only a few extracts from it. " There are here thirty-thousand families common in faith with us, and they pray God for your prosperity......Our province in which the Christians dwell is called Malabar, and has about twenty cities... In all these, Christians live and churches have been built...... About twenty Portuguese live in the city of Cannanor. When we arrived from Ormuz at Cannanor, we presented ourselves to them, said *that we were Christians and explained our condition and rank.* They received us with

---

[1] Travancore State Manual, vol. II, p. 60.
[2] Op.cit. pp. 588-596.

great joy, gave us beautiful garments, and twenty drachmas of gold, and for Christ's sake they honoured our journey more than it deserved. We remained with them *for two and a half months*, and they ordered us that on a fixed day we also should perform the Holy Mysteries, *i.e.*, should offer the Oblation.

"They had prepared a proper place for prayer, which they called the Oratory, and their priests offer sacrifice every day and complete the Holy Oblation ; for that is their custom and rite. Whereof on Nosardel Sunday, *after their priests had celebrated, we also were admitted and performed the holy sacri-fice, and it was greatly pleasing in their eyes.*[1] We started thence and arrived among our Christians who dwell at a distance of eight days from that place."

From this passage, in which Mr. Mackenzie seems to find his strongest evidence for the Nestorianism of the St. Thomas Christians, it is not difficult to establish that these bishops and the people they report about are Catholics. For it cannot be maintained that the Portuguese priests at Cannanor, after they had said Mass, would allow these foreign bishops to offer their Oblation on the sacred altar if they were Nestorians. How could they, moreover, hear it through and tell the bishops that they were greatly pleased with the Oblation, unless they were perfectly sure that these prelates who were offering the Holy my-steries in a language unknown to them were Catholic bishops of an Oriental Rite in communion with Rome, and that, as such, there would be nothing objectionable in allowing them the use of the sacred altar and in being present for the Oblation ? This must necessarily be the explanation since these bishops had made known to the Portuguese their condition and rank and had remained with them for two and a half months—time amply sufficient to detect their heresy if any. Moreover, the fact that Jacob Abuna, who, as we shall see, was a Catholic bishop praised as such by St. Francis Xavier, was one of these bishops, leads us to conclude that the four others his companions were also

---

[1] " Et sacerdotes eorum quotidie sacram conficiunt Oblationem et sacrifi-cant : hic enim est mos et ritus eorum. Quamobrem Dominica die Nusard-Eil, postquam sacerdos eorum celebrasset, nos quoque admissi fuimus et sacrum fecimus : et placuit valde oculis eorum." Giamil, pp. 594-596.

Catholic bishops. And as to Mar John, who was administering alone the Indian Church when these four bishops came, De Souza says that he lived in the church at Cranganore and that he raised to life the sacristan of that Church who had died from a fall. Francis Roz s.j., Archbishop of Angamale for a short time, read this event in an old Chaldæan manuscript.[1] It would further be noticed that, in this report submitted by the bishops, there is nothing to show that either they or the people were Nestorians. Hence this catena of testimonies forces us to conclude that these bishops, the people to whom they came, as well as the Patriarch who sent them, were all Catholics.

It was only on Vasco-de-Gama's second voyage to India in 1502 that the Christian community in Malabar came under his personal observation. The interview he had with the Christians may be given in the words of the " Asia Portuguzae[2] ":— " Here (at Cochin) Don Vasco received ambassadors who said they came from some Christian inhabitants of that neighbouring country, the metropolis whereof was Cranganore, and they were to the number ef 30,000, that St. Thomas had preached to their forefathers, that they were subject to the Patriarch of Armenia, that they were infested by the pagans, *that they knew he was an officer of the most Catholic King of Europe to whom they submitted themselves* delivering into his hands the Rod of Justice. This rod was red, about the length of a sceptre, ends tipt with silver with three bells at the top. They were despatched with hopes of a powerful assistance." Another interesting incident given by the same author shows that, at this time, the Christians had images in their churches, and so they could not have been Nestorians, for the veneration of images is strictly forbidden to the Nestorians. The Portuguese were taken to see one of the churches of these Christians. " In the middle was a round chapel of good structure with brass gates ; within it was the statue of a woman, which, by reason of the darkness, could not be perfectly discovered. The Portuguese looking upon it and asking what it was, the Malabars answered aloud and with a joyful

---

[1] Oriente Conquistado, vol. II. p. 69, Lisbon, 1710.

[2] Manuel de Faria y Sousa, translated by John Stevens t. 1, p. 67, London, 1695.

reverence, 'Mary, Mary, Mary,' and prostrated themselves on the ground. Our men did the same judging that to be the image of Our Lady, nor were they deceived, for it could be no other, those people many ages before having professed Christianity."[1]

In 1504 Suarez de Menezes captured Cranganore and ordered it to be burnt. " The work of destruction had begun when some Christian inhabitants of the place came and entreated him to desist, representing that within the city were several churches dedicated to the Virgin and the Apostles which would be destroyed. The conflagration was therefore stopped."[2] This fact, if examined in the light of the religious intolerance that was the characteristic note of those days, plainly shows that the Christians to whom the Portuguese behaved so kindly could not have been of any other religious denomination except their own, *i.e.*, they were Catholics.

In 1530, John D'Albuquerque who had come to Goa as the first Portuguese Bishop, sent to Cochin a Franciscan, Father Vincent de Lagos, to educate the Syrian Christians. Father Vincent opened a seminary for the Syrian youths who wished to study for the priesthood.

The great missionary St. Francis Xavier set foot on Indian soil, 6th May 1542. We are concerned here not with his varied missionary activities, but with some of his letters which prove very clearly that Francis Xavier was amply convinced of the orthodoxy of the St. Thomas Christians.

In a letter of the 14th January 1549, he writes to Ignatius Loyola[3] :—" Fra Vincenzo has founded a really fine Seminary where quite as many as a hundred native students are maintained and are formed in piety and learning......He has asked me again and again to provide a priest of the Society who may teach grammar to the students of the seminary and preach to the inmates and the people on Sundays and festivals. There is reason for this, because, *besides the Portuguese inhabitants of the place, there are a great many Christians* living in sixty villages

---

[1] Manuel de Faria y Sousa, translated by John Stevens, t. 1, p. 46, London, 1695.

[2] Francis Day. Op. cit. p. 94.

[3] Life and Letters of St. Francis Xavier by Father Coleridge s.j., vol. II, pp. 73-74, London, 1872.

in the neighbourhood, *descended from those whom St. Thomas made Christians.* The students of this seminary are of the highest nobility. In this town (Cranganore) there are two churches, one of St. Thomas, one of St. James. Fra Vincenzo, whom I have mentioned, hopes much that you will get each of them *a plenary indulgence* once a year from the Holy Father, on the feasts of St. Thomas and St. James and the seven days after each. This would be *to increase the piety of the* natives who are descended from the converts of St. Thomas and are called *Christians of St. Thomas.*"

After an interval of only fourteen days Francis Xavier wrote to Father Simon Rodriguez a similar letter[1]:—"There (at Cranganore) there is a fine college which was built by Fra Vincenzo, the companion of the Bishop, where as many as a hundred youths, children of the native Christians, who are called Christians of St. Thomas, are educated; for there are sixty villages of these Christians of St. Thomas around the town, and from them the students I speak of are derived. At Cranganore there are two churches; one of St. Thomas, which is very piously frequented by the Christians of St. Thomas, and another of St. James adjoining the college. Fra Vincenzo wishes very much that *indulgences should be obtained* for both these churches *to be a consolation for these Christians and to increase their piety.* So I beg you very much to procure, either through our people at Rome or through the Pontifical Nuncio at Lisbon, a yearly plenary indulgence for each, beginning from the Vigil of St James and the Vigil of St. Thomas respectively, and lasting for the eight following days. I would have this indulgence offered only to those who may have duly approached *the Sacraments of Penance and holy Communion,* and then piously and devoutly visited these churches at Cranganore."

In a letter[2] to John III of Portugal, dated 26th January 1549, Francis Xavier makes mention of Mar Jacob, the only one still living of the five Bishops who had been sent by the Patri-

---

[1] Life and Letters of St. Francis Xavier by Father Coleridge: vol. II. pp. 89-90, London, 1872.
[2] Ibid. pp. 82-83.

arch in 1502. "*It is now five and forty years that a certain Armenian Bishop, by name Jacob Abuna, has served God and Your Highness in this country.* He *is a man* who is about as dear to God on account of his virtue and holiness as he is neglected and despised by your Highness and in general by all who have any power in India. God thus rewards his great deserts Himself, and does not think us worthy of the honour of being the instruments whom He uses to console His servants. ......While I have been writing this, I have seemed to myself to be serving and doing a favour not so much to that pious Bishop as to your Highness......For at present *your Highness is very greatly in want of the goodwill and intercession of a man very acceptable to God as he is*......This Bishop very greatly deserves such treatment on this account if on no other—that *he has spent much labour in attending to the Christians of St. Thomas,* and now in his all but decrepit old age, he conforms himself most obediently, to all the rites and customs of our holy Mother the Roman Church........I would urge your Highness to write it (him a letter) full of all manner of expressions of your favour, esteem and affection."

These letters of St. Francis Xavier are very important documents to prove the orthodoxy of the St. Thomas Christians in those days. In the first of the three letters Francis Xavier requests St. Ignatius to provide a priest of the society to teach grammar to the students of the Seminary, and to preach to the people on Sundays and festivals; for he sees the important *rôle* this institution, which was unique in India at the time, would play in educating for the priesthood the sons of the highest nobility, through whose instrumentality the whole of Malabar could be converted to the Christian Faith. He asks St. Ignatius to obtain for each of the churches a plenary indulgence once a year from the Holy Father, and that, in order to increase the piety of the natives who are descended from the converts of St. Thomas and are called Christians of St. Thomas. It cannot for a moment be believed that St. Francis would interest himself so much as to write two letters to two different persons to obtain a plenary indulgence—something foreign to the Nestorian or any other faith except the Catholic religion—for the Church of St. Thomas, to increase the piety of these Christians, if they were not already Catholics. Hence the reasonable deduction, and the one strongly held by St. Francis himself, is that the Church of St. Thomas was Catholic, and so were all the St. Thomas Christians who very piously frequented it and sent their sons to the seminary to be educated for the priesthood.

The third letter of St. Francis is also very important. We have seen that, of the five Bishops who were in Malabar in 1504, there was, by the year 1549, only one still living, and that was Mar Jacob, or Jacob Abuna. This letter is important as giving Francis Xavier's opinion of the Faith of this Bishop after he had been acquainted with him for a period of seven years. It should be noted that we have not a shred of document to prove that this Bishop had ever changed his religious convictions, or abjured by word of mouth or in writing any error or heresy he may have so long held; such a document is not forthcoming in the writings of even the stoutest upholders of the Nestorianism of the St. Thomas Christians. We are consequently justified in asserting that the faith of this bishop was the same during a course of forty-five years from 1504 - 1549, that in the interval it had not undergone any modification whatever, that this was also the Faith of the Bishops, his companions, who started with him and who conjointly submitted the report, that this was the same Faith as that of the Patriarch who sent him and his companions, and finally that this Faith was exactly the same as that of the thirty-thousand families of St. Thomas Christians about whom the report was submitted. Consequently we see the importance of this letter. Let us examime it carefully. "It is now five and forty years that a certain Armenian Bishop by name Jacob Abuna has served (*inservit*[1]) God and your Highness in this country. He is dear to God on account of his virtue and holiness." St. Francis would not surely have written of this virtuous and holy Bishop as serving God for forty-five years, if he had, during this time, been a Nestorian, and he would not have counted these years as spent in the

---

[1] The correct translation of *inservit* would give ' serves.'

service of God if the Bishop had passed them as a Nestorian heretic. Moreover, it is not likely that Francis Xavier would have said that a heretic bishop was very dear to God, and would have asked the King of Portugal to earn for himself the intercession before God of a heretic Bishop. Further, the Saint himself admits that the holy Bishop conformed himself most obediently to the customs and rites of the Roman Church. Hence there cannot be two opinions on the issue that Mar Jacob was a Catholic Bishop.

The testimony of orthodoxy which these letters proclaim, says Mr. Mackenzie, cannot be easily explained away. I assert that these letters and the whole attitude of St. Francis Xavier and the *early* missionaries towards these Christians—treating them so kindly, providing them a Seminary for the education of their sons for the priesthood, and always referring to them as the Christians of St. Thomas and never once as Nestorians,—place the orthodoxy of these Christians on a very solid basis, and establish in the clearest terms that these Christians of St. Thomas were Catholics under the jurisdiction of a Catholic Patriarch who was obedient to Rome.

In 1549, the aged Mar Jacob died, and for the next six years the Syrian Church was without a Bishop. Meanwhile some changes were taking place in the Patriarchate of Babylon.

On the death of Simon Mama, *of good memory*, in 1551, many Chaldæans, dissatisfied with the custom that had grown up of electing as Patriarch only candidates of the Bar-mama family, chose John Sulaka, a pious monk, and sent him to Rome. Pope Julins III consecrated him as Patriarch of the East. He returned home, but was put to death by the Turks in 1554. His successor, Ebedjesus followed his example, visited Rome, and assisted at the last session of the Council of Trent. He consecrated Mar Joseph, a brother of John Sulaka, as Archbishop of the Syrian Christians on the Malabar Coast.

As a Catholic prelate of the Syrian Rite sent by the Chaldæan Patriarch, Mar Joseph refused to ordain the students of the seminary at Cranganore who belonged to the Syrian

Rite, but who had not been taught the Syriac language.[1] This refusal lost him the favour and earned the ill-will of the Portuguese, who, from this time forward, never ceased to persecute him and his successors. Finding no reasonable grounds to send him out of the country, they had recourse to their favourite weapon—a weapon, as we shall see, so often used with such disastrous effects—that the Bishop taught the Nestorian heresy. Before long he was taken to Goa and thence deported to Portugal. There he made so favourable an impression on Cardinal Don Henry and others, that he was naturally sent back to govern his people.[2] The Portuguese authorities at Goa, however, did not allow him to proceed to his diocese, but detained him at Bassein.

When Mar Joseph was deported to Portugal, the Patriarch, informed of these events, immediately sent Mar Abraham as Bishop of the Syrian Christians He escaped the vigilance of the 'argus-eyed and many-handed' agents of the Portuguese, by travelling in disguise and through circuitous roads, and arrived among the Syrian Christians. The Portuguese, deeming this a good opportunity to create dissension and discord in the community and win over one party to their interests, released Mar Joseph from his detention at Bassein and sent him to his diocese. Soon after, however, Mar Abraham fell into their hands, and was shipped off to Portugal. He managed to escape at Mozambique, made his way to the Persian Gulf, and presented himself before the Patriarch relating to him his experiences in India. He was sent to Pope Pius IV, who requested the Patriarch to consecrate Mar Abraham as Archbishop of Angamale, and to divide the Christians of St. Thomas in Malabar between Mar Abraham and Mar Joseph.[3]

Let us first consider the career of Mar Joseph. He prescribed vestments in the Roman style for priests when saying Mass. He introduced the host and wine as used by the Portuguese, whereas the Syrian priests were till then making use of fermented bread and wine in accordance with the customs of

---

[1] Travancore State Manual, vol. II. p. 162.
[2] Ibid.
[3] Giamil. Op. cit. pp. 69-71.

all Oriental Churches. These innovations notwithstanding, the Portuguese accused him a second time of heresy, and on such an unfounded charge, they reported him to Cardinal Don Henry who placed the case before Pope Pius V, and requested him to empower the Archbishop of Goa to enquire into the doctrines of Mar Joseph. In 1567, Mar Joseph attended the First Provincial Council of Goa, and the charge of heresy being framed against him, he was sent to Portugal and thence to Rome. There, after an examination by the Pope and Cardinals, they were convinced that the charge of heresy was unfounded. Recognising his great learning, piety and other virtues, they resolved to create him a Cardinal,[1] when his unexpected and suspicious death[2] put an end to any such project.

In 1568, Mar Abraham arrived at Goa with credentials from the Pope and the Patriarch, in which the Pope requested the Archbishop of Goa to receive Mar Abraham as a brother. The arrival of Mar Abraham disconcerted the Portuguese, for it threatened to subvert their designs, and they determined to prevent his return to the coast. "*The Archbishop*, therefore, *took upon him to declare the Pope's briefs to be null and void, as* having been obtained under false pretences [3]," and Mar Abraham was confined in the Dominican Convent at Goa. He managed to escape, however, and reached his diocese. In 1578, he received a summons to attend the Provincial Council of Goa. He refused on the ground that he was responsible only to his Patriarch [4], and that he had been ill-treated and twice thrown into prison at Goa. To this effect also he induced the Raja of

---

1 "Before Mar Joseph could undertake a new voyage to India, he died at Rome on the eve of his being made a Cardinal." *Asiatic Researches*, vol. VII. p. 373, Calcutta 1801. Oriente Conquistado which is bitterly hostile to this Bishop admits (II, 275) that in Rome "they deemed him worthy of a Cardinal's hat.

2 "The abrupt manner in which Gouvea closes his account of this bishop, tends to awaken suspicion respecting the causes of his death." Hough. Op. cit. vol, I. p. 260.

3 Ibid. p. 276.

4 "Mar Abraham complained to the Pope, ' that the Fathers of the Society of Jesus and the Latin Portuguese ' tried to withdraw him from obedience to the Chaldæan Patriarch, and to persuade him to demand the *pallium* directly from the Pope. In this way, they sought to compel him to conform to the Latin Rite." Catholic Encyclopædia, vol. III Article ' Chaldæan Christians, ' IV Malabar Christians.' p. 561.

Cochin to write to the Pope.[1] Two years later the Pope wrote to the Archbishop of Goa, requesting him to "receive kindly our venerable brother the Archbishop of Angamale, and so to contrive that here and elsewhere he may experience your humanity and love[2]." The Pope also wrote to the King of Portugal recommending to his Majesty "the venerable brother the Archbishop of Angamale who had been grievously vexed by some persons," and asking him to "order the Viceroy and Governors of India to take steps that he be not oppressed with any injury."[3]

For the next fourteen years the relations between Mar Abraham and the Portuguese were normal, though not very friendly. At this time three Syrians, Abraham, Joseph and George Raisbander wrote a valuable letter to the Pope in which they expose the state of the Indian Church left without a sufficient number of Bishops, and *request the Holy See to send letters to the Patriarch asking him to consecrate five Bishops for this Church as has been done by the Patriarch from the very beginning.*[4] In 1579, Mar Abraham requested the *pallium* from the Pope, and there is a Memorandum on the subject in the Vatican Library.[5] In 1584, Mar Abraham informed the Pope that, in virtue of the powers granted him by the Patriarch, he had appointed Archdeacon George, Bishop-elect of Palur, to be his coadjutor and successor, and requests the Pope to confirm the appointment.[6]

In 1578, there arrived on this coast, a Bishop Mar Simon, calling himself the Metropolitan of the St. Thomas Christians. The best authorities are agreed that he was a Nestorian Bishop. He fixed his seat at Caduthuruthi and gathered some adherents. But the letter of Pope Gregory XIII, dated March 1580, sent on the recommendation of Mar Abraham to the Syrian Christians, "to be obedient in the Lord to Mar Abraham, your Archbishop, and to *George the Bishop of Palur,* and in sincerity

---

[1] Giamil. Op. cit. pp. 75-76.
[2] Ibid. p. 604.
[3] Ibid. p. 606.
[4] Ibid. pp. 85-86.
[5] Ibid. pp. 74-75.
[6] Ibid. p. 100.

f faith and simplicity of manners, persevere and live in the
nity of our Holy Mother, the Church,[1]" put an end to any
rospect the Bishop had of influencing any considerable section
f the people. As resolved in the third Council of Goa, 1585,
e was soon arrested and sent through Goa to Portugal and
hence to Rome. Before his arrest, however, he managed to
ppoint Jacob, a Syrian Priest, as his Vicar-General. Mar Jacob
ollowed in the wake of his Superior, taught Nestorian doc-
rines, and continued the schism for a space of twelve more
ears.[2]

The Society of Jesus had been allowed by Mar Abraham in
574 to work in his diocese. In 1581 they had opened a
ollege, built a church and set up a printing press in Vaipicotta.
'wo years later, at their instance, Mar Abraham convoked a
liocesan synod in which *Mass was said in both Syriac and Latin.*[3]
n 1584, a seminary was added to the college, and as both Syriac
nd Latin were taught in it, it was much frequented by the
ons of the St. Thomas Christians. In a letter one of the
'esuit Fathers wrote to the Pope, he praises Mar Abraham
nd Archdeacon George, and suggests the latter as the fittest
aan for the administration of the diocese after the death of
Mar Abraham.[4]

In the Provincial Council of Goa in 1585, Mar Abraham
vas asked to re-ordain some of the priests he had ordained
ccording to the Chaldæan rite, because the Portuguese con-
idered that the ordination of priests with the imposition of
ands and with the *empty chalice and paten* was invalid, whereas
his has been the recognised practice of Oriental Churches at
ll times.

The Council of Goa, in the 7th decree of the 3rd session,
ad ordered the translation of the Latin Mass into Syriac for
he use of the St. Thomas Christians. Mar Abraham, as we have
een, had, at the earnest request of the Portuguese, consented
o some changes in the ceremonies of the Mass, of ordination,

---

[1] Giamil. p. 608.
[2] Trav. State Manual, vol. II, p. 169.
[3] Ibid. p. 170.
[4] Giamil. Op. cit. pp. 79-82.

and in the use of unleavened bread and wine of grapes. This
he had done without consulting his Patriarch. The Patriarch,
therefore, called upon him to submit an explanation of his
conduct. Mar Abraham answered that he did these things at
the insistence of the Portuguese "who were over his head as a
hammer over an anvil."

This explanation, Gouvea mistakenly says, was demanded,
not by the Catholic but by the Nestorian Patriarch.[1] And the
statement has been repeated without the slightest modification
and without any examination into the details of the issue by
Dr. Geddes, and it is to be found faithfully reproduced in Hough,
and is accepted as a historical fact by Day, Whitehouse and
all later historians.

After this warning from the Catholic Patriarch, Mar
Abraham refused in 1590 to ordain the clerical students of the
Vaipicotta Seminary,[2] because he was asked to ordain them
according to the Latin Ritual. Two years later he refused to
attend the Fourth Council of Goa. Thereupon the Portuguese
sent unfavourable reports of his conduct to the Pope, accusing
him of Nestorian heresy. But Mar Abraham had now finished
his life-work. Peter Jarri, s.J.,[3] testifies that 'Mar Abraham
loved the Jesuits, invited the Rector of Vaipicotta to his death-
bed, committed his flock to the care of the Jesuits, and commanded all his clergy to obey them and regard the Pope as
their own Patriarch.' He died in 1597.

Thus we see that Mar Joseph and Mar Abraham lived and
died as Catholic Bishops, and yet historians have invariably
written of them as Nestorian bishops.

---

[1] Tr. State Manual, vol. II, p. 171.
[2] Ibid. p. 171.
[3] Cited in the 'Orthodoxy of the St. Thomas Christians', p. 50, Kottayam,
1904.

CHAPTER IV

The Synod of Diamper 1599.

We intend in this chapter to point out briefly that some of the decrees of the Synod of Diamper, which have been presumably drawn up to expose and correct the so-called Nestorian errors of the St. Thomas Christians, as well as the events that preceded the Synod itself, are the best and most obvious proofs that these Christians were Catholics even before the Synod.

In the year 1594, Father Alexius de Menezes, a young man of thirty-five, was appointed Archbishop of Goa. The following year he landed in India. The authenticity of the two Briefs of Clement VIII by which the Archbishop claimed jurisdiction over the Malabar Church, is very doubtful. For it is said in one of them that the Pope commanded him upon the death of the Archbishop Mar Abraham "to take possession of this Church and bishopric, so as not to suffer any Bishop or prelate coming from Babylon to enter therein as has hitherto been the custom."[1]

We have seen, however, that Mar Abraham had informed Pope Gregory XIII that, acting upon the powers he had received from his Patriarch, he had appointed Archdeacon George, Bishop-elect of Palur, to be his coadjutor and successor and had requested the Pope to confirm this appointment. That the Pope had granted the request, is clear from the fact that His Holiness, when warning the people against Mar Simeon, had asked them "to be obedient also to George, the Bishop of Palur."[2] Hence it seems rather strange that the Pope should have now empowered the Archbishop "to take possession of this bishopric" without at least informing the Archdeacon of the setting aside of his legitimate and just claims. The opinion that the Archbishop was not sufficiently authorised by the Pope, is confirmed by the words of the former,[3] "that the same was incumbent on us of right—the said Church having no chaplain

[1] Hough. Op. cit. vol. II. p. 2.
[2] Giamil. Op. cit. p. 68.
[3] Hough. Op. cit. vol. II. p. 2.

to take care of it during the vacancy of the see—as Metropolitan and Primate of this and all the other Churches of the Indies and the Oriental countries." He claims to be *by right* the Metropolitan and Primate of all the Churches of the Indies and the East. Consequently he does not respect or pay any regard to the time-honoured authority and ancient prerogative of the Patriarch of Babylon over the Malabar Church. He throws to the winds the order of Pope Pius IV[1] "to preserve inviolate the jurisdiction of the Patriarch and of the Bishops he may appoint over the Indian Church," and to find some plausible reason for this usurpation, he labours hard to show that he took charge of the Archdiocese, because "it was vacant, and there was no one to take care of it during the vacancy." How contrary this statement is to facts we have seen, for the Bishop of Palur had the right of succession. The Archbishop, moreover, knew that both Mar Abraham and the Bishop of Palur had applied to the Patriarch for another Bishop. In response a Bishop and a Priest were sent. But the ever active agents of the Archbishop were so closely watching all the ports, that they could not elude their vigilance and were discovered at Ormuz and sent back. Thus Menezes did his utmost to make the see fall vacant, that he might with some justification take possession of it.

Not long after, Archbishop Menezes appointed Father Francis Roz, a Spaniard, to administer the Malabar diocese. But this appointment was too glaring a violation of the Archdeacon's claims to be tamely submitted to by the Syrians. As remarked by Whitehouse[2], "the community was so thoroughly roused, and so strong was the feeling excited, that the Syrians would no longer permit any Latin priest to officiate in their churches." Toned down by this resistance, the Council at Goa became more prudent, and at their instance, the appointment of Father Roz was cancelled and the Archdeacon was reinstated in his rights. The historian Hough[3] is at a loss to understand how the Council

---

[1] Giamil. Op. cit. p. 72.   [2] Op. cit. p. 92.

[3] Op. cit. vol. I. p. 301. The same surpise is shared by D'Orsey, who says: "The Archbishop held a meeting at Goa concerning the Syrian Church, and the result was that, in spite of the Pope's orders that none but a Roman Catholic should be appointed, it was deemed expedient to nominate the Archdeacon." Op. cit. p. 188.

at Goa and the Archbishop, in spite of the Pope's orders "that no one should be placed in charge of the diocese who was not of the Roman communion," could appoint the Archdeacon. The simple answer is that Archdeacon George was a Catholic, and consequently there was, in this case at least, no violation of the of the Pope's orders.

After this impolitic move on the part of the Archbishop and the Portuguese, their ultimate object became very plain to the Syrians. They understood that the whole policy of the Portuguese for which they had been working for more than a century, was to substitute the Latin Liturgy for the Syriac,[1] and if they succeeded in this attempt, they could exercise complete jurisdiction over the Malabar Church, for then the Syrians could no more be subject to the Patriarch of Babylon who would be of a different rite from theirs. To cloak this ultimate object, they put forward the favourite plea that if these people followed the Syriac Liturgy and submitted to the jurisdiction of the Chaldæan Patriarch, they might revert to their Nestorian errors. A letter[2] dated Dec. 19, 1597, written by the Archbishop himself to the Patriarch of Jesusalem who was then at Rome, is our authority for the above statement. "The priests with many people held a meeting and took an oath that in case His Holiness appointed a Syrian bishop, they would obey him, but if he sends a Latin bishop (this is the important point), they will consider what course they would adopt." Now, if the people, priests and Archdeacon were Nestorians, how could they obey a Syrian Bishop appointed by the Pope, for the Bishop so appointed could only be a Catholic Syrian Bishop? It is evident, therefore, that the people, priests and Archdeacon were all Catholics who wished to cling to their Syrian Rite and were ready to submit to a Syrian Catholic Bishop appointed by the Pope. This conclusion is all the more evident from the remaining part of the sentence, for even if His Holiness appointed a

---

[1] Catholic Encyclopædia, vol. III, p. 561, Article: 'Chaldæan Christians'. "The clergy of Goa, tried to annex them (the St. Thomas Christians) by a process of latinization, and the Jesuits, successors of St. Francis Xavier, followed a similar policy, but with much moderation and practical sense."

[2] Travancore State Manual, vol. II, p.

Latin Bishop, they do not say they will disobey him, but "will consider what course to adopt,"—perhaps petition His Holiness to remove the Latin Bishop and give them one of their own rite. The letter continues, "*an order must be given to the Bishop* [who is to be appointed] *that he may extinguish little by little the Syrian language which is not natural. His priests should learn the Latin language, because the Syrian language is the channel through which all that heresy flows. A good administrator ought to replace Syrian by Latin.* Above all, it is most important that the Bishop be a suffragan of this city, as is at present the Bishop of Cochin, his nearest neighbour." This is plain and unmistakable language and entirely corroborates the conclusion I have arived at above.

On February 1st 1599, Archbishop Menezes landed in Cochin. He at once applied for co-operation from the governor Antonio de Noronha and the Hindu Raja of Cochin, promising to procure for the latter the title of 'Brother-in-Arms' of Portugal.[1] By thus winning over the civil powers, by threatening to excommunicate the Archdeacon, by ordaining a majority of clergy who would zealously lend their valuable aid to the reforms in the Chaldæan Liturgy, and by cajoling those already in Holy Orders, and conciliating the chief of the laity, he prepared them all to listen obsequiously to the decrees which he had already composed for their acceptance.[2] One thing, however, they unanimously agreed in declining to give up. This was the ancient custom of praying in the Syrian tongue, declaring that they would rather sacrifice their lives than pray in Latin.[3] Menezes, seeing that on this point they would not yield, conceded the question. This concession, coupled with the fact that there was merely a change of jurisdiction, a substitution of Latin bishops for the Syrian, and not a change of doctrines, explains what seems to be incomprehensible to Milne

---

[1, 2] Vol. I, p. 462 : "An assembly convened under such circumstances cannot rightly be called a synod, the object of which was always understood to be freely and fully to discuss the ecclesiastical affairs of a given province. Whereas nothing was further from the intention of Menezes than to allow of any discussion whatever, having already determined all the matters to be brought before the Assembly, and secured their concurrence."

[3] Francis Day. Op. cit. p. 231.

Rae,[1] who says :—"History searches in vain for their martyrs, their Hamiltons and Wisharts, their Ridleys and Latimers."

The Archdeacon had an interview[2] with the Archbishop, in which the former protested that it would be base on his part to desert the Patriarch who had been from time immemorial the eccleciastical head of the Malabar Church. He agreed, however, to the convocation of a Synod, but urged that Menezes, in his tour through the country as a foreign prelate, should abstain from all essentially episcopal acts, as these would be very hurtful to the legitimate and just claims of the Chaldæan Patriarch and should confine his ministrations to preaching and blessing the people.

Angamale was to have had the honour of giving its name to the Synod, but for interested motives, Diamper, commonly known as Udiamperur, within an easy distance of Cochin and its Portuguese garrison, was finally chosen, and the 20th June was fixed as the auspicious day. We are not concerned here with the details of this historic Synod, which may be read in Gouvea, Geddes, Hough, and other authors. But we are constrained to make a few observations on certain decrees of the Synod, which clearly attest and confirm the fact that the Syrian Church in Malabar was Catholic before the Synod, and as regards making it Catholic, the Synod was a "mere farce,"[3] for this Church was united to that of Rome through the Catholic Patriarch of Babylon.

It must, however, in justice to the Archbishop and to all who had any part in convening the Synod, be admitted that some of its Sessions and Decrees were very useful and praiseworthy.[4] The Christians were forbidden to sell arrack, to join their Hindu neighbours in the sham fights which took place in the month of August during the Hindu festival of Onam; they were not to resort to witches and fortune-tellers, to consult them about such things as lucky and unlucky days, or to submit at the command of their Hindu rulers to such ordeals as

[1] Op. cit. p. 246.
[2] Whitehouse. Op. cit p 101
[3] Hough. Op. cit vol. I p. 462
[4] Whitehouse. Op cit. pp.114-115

handling bars of red-hot iron, thrusting the hand into boiling oil, or swimming across a river infested with crocodiles. They were also prohibited from observing the Nambudhiri custom of the separation of a mother from both religious and domestic ceremonies for forty days after the birth of a boy and for eighty days after the birth of a girl.

These few salutary reforms, however, were obtained at a very heavy cost, the cost involved in the loss of a very old Liturgy, and in the substitution of a new rite, the Syro-Malabar Rite, different from both the Chaldæan and Latin Rites, with Syriac as the liturgical language into which most of the Latin Missal and ceremonies have been translated with additions taken from the old Liturgy, and with certain peculiarities preserved from the ancient rite, which, in the minds of the authors of the Synod, did not savour of Nestorianism. The present Syro-Malabar Liturgy is a sad contrast in its new form, after it had passed through the ordeal of the Synod, to the former beautiful and ancient Syro-Chaldæan Liturgy.

Now let us examine some of the decrees of the Synod. Here is an extract from the circular[1] of Menezes convening the Synod, which speaks for itself:—" We were also moved by the piety of the people, and *the mercy God had shown them in having preserved so many thousand souls in the Faith of our Lord Jesus Christ, from the time that the Holy Apostle Thomas had preached to them until this day*, notwithstanding their having lived among so many heathens and been scattered in diverse places, their churches and all belonging to them, having been always subject to idolatrous kings and princes and encompassed with idols and pagodas, and that without holding any correspondence with any other Christians before the coming of the Portuguese into these parts; we being likewise desirous *that the labours of the Holy Apostle, St. Thomas, which still remained among them,* should not be lost through want of sound doctrine.;.....did determine and prepare to go in person to take possession of the said bishopric." In the same circular, we read, "*we do, therefore, by virtue of holy obedience and upon pain of ex-commu-*

---

[1] Hough, vol. II, p. 2.

nication, [*latæ sententiæ*], command the Revd. the Archdeacon of this diocese and all the other priests of the same, that shall not be hindered by age or some other just impediment, to be present at the said town of Diamper, there with us to celebrate a diocesan Synod, conformable to the holy canons............*We do under the same precept and censure* command all Christians in all towns and villages of this bishopric......to choose four of the most honourable, conscientious and experienced persons among them to come in their name to the said Synod with sufficient powers to approve, sign, confirm and consult in their name, so as to oblige themselves thereby to comply with whatsoever shall be determined at the Synod." The impression which a careful reading of these passages and the whole circular leaves on the mind of an impartial person, is naturally that the Archbishop is calling upon a Catholic people, under the heaviest penalty of the Church, *viz.*, that of cutting them off from the communion of the Faithful in case any one should willingly absent himself from the Synod. These threats of ex-communication would otherwise be meaningless. Moreover, the Archbishop himself expresses in the plainest language that the Syrian Christians were Catholics before the Synôd, for he says that the mercy of God has preserved many thousand souls in the Faith of Jesus Christ, from the time of the preaching of the Apostle until this day, and that the labours of the Apostle still remained among them. Hence, on the strength of this one assertion, we might boldly declare that the St. Thomas Christians were Catholics before the Synod of Diamper.

But we have still other extracts to be culled from the decrees of the Synod. The fourth decree of the first session contains the following passage,[1] "We do admonish and command *all Christians* as well ecclesiastics as seculars gathered together in this place *to confess their sins* with a true contrition for them, *and all priests to say Mass, and others to receive the Most Holy Sacrament of the altar*, beseeching our Lord with humble and devout prayers for good success to all that shall be treated of in this Synod, to which intent there shall be *two*

---

[1] Hough. vol. II. p. 517.

solemn Masses said in the church every day during the session of the Synod, *one of the Latins to the Holy Spirit, and the other of the Syrians to our Lady. . . . .* They shall likewise, Latins as well as Syrians, every day after sunset, sing the solemn litanies of the Church with a commemoration of our Lady, for the good intention of the Synod." It goes without saying that Dom Menezes would not and could not allow the Syrian priests to celebrate Mass, and the Syrian people to receive the Holy Communion, if they were Nestorian heretics, and especially if, as is asserted, their Taksas[1] contained heretical passages. *These recommendations were made on the first day of the Synod, whereas* the so-called *corrections in the Taksas were made only on the third day,* in the ninth decree of the third session. It was indispensable to correct the Missals before allowing them to be used in the Mass, in order that the Holy Sacrifice might not be performed with heretical Taksas. Further, if the Syrian Christians were Nestorians, how could the sacrilegious Masses of their priests, and the unworthy Communions of the people, contribute in the least to the good success of the Synod ?

Again, in the profession of Faith[2] read to the Archdeacon by the Portuguese, we find:—"I do also promise, vow and swear to God on this cross and these Holy Gospels, never to receive into this Church and Bishopric of the Serra (mountains), any bishop, archbishop, prelate, pastor or governor whatsoever, *but what shall be immediately appointed by the Holy Apostolical See and the Bishop of Rome,* and that, whomsoever he shall appoint, I will receive and obey as my true pastor, *without expecting any message or having any further dependence upon the Patriarch of Babylon.*" It is quite manifest, therefore, that the bishops of this Church were till now appointed only indirectly by the Pope, they being in the first place immediately and directly appointed by the Patriarch of Babylon who was in communion with the Apostolic See of Rome. But now this arrangement is altered and the Syrian Church is placed directly under the Pope, who appoints the necessary bishops to it,

---

[1] The Syrian Missals (books used in the Mass) are called Taksas.
[2] Hough, vol. II, p. 523.

through the Archbishop of Goa. This meaning of the passage seems to be clear from the words "without expecting any message" as to whether the Patriarch agrees to the altered conditions or puts in a protest to the Holy See against the deprivation by the Portuguese of a part of his Patriarchate wherein he had so long exercised complete jurisdiction, and "without having any further dependence upon the Patriarch of Babylon" whom the people are called upon to condemn, reject and anathematise as being a Nestorian schismatic and heretic.

Here I may be permitted to bring together a short list of the Chaldæan Patriarchs from 1490 - 1600, with a special view to bring out the fact that the Patriarch at the time of the Synod was a Catholic, and that the Portuguese were mistaken in styling him a Nestorian. We have seen that in 1490 Mar Simon V sent two bishops, and that his successor Mar Elias had despatched three more bishops to India. We have read the report they submitted to the Patriarch in 1504, in which they say that they were admitted by the Portuguese to say Mass in their churches. We have in a previous section established the orthodoxy of these Bishops, and consequently of the two Patriarchs who sent them to India.

We may infer that Simon Mama, the predecessor of John Sulaka who ruled the Church about 1550, was a Catholic, because, as can be read in Giamil, the Pope uses the significant and orthodox expression " *of good memory*,"[1] when speaking of this Patriarch, and surely there is not a single instance where the Pope has made use of this appellation when speaking of a schismatic or heretical Bishop or Patriarch. Moreover, one of the five MSS books of the Chaldæan Pontifical in the Vatican Library was transcribed in Mesopotamia in 1529, with the translation of some portion from the Latin Pontifical by the Patriarch Mar Simon Mama.[2] On these grounds we infer he was a Catholic Patriarch.

---

[1] Samuel Giamil, p. 24.
[2] Asseman. Op. cit. t. 4, p. 378.

The orthodoxy of his successor John Sulaka, who assumed the reins of government in 1551, has not so far been called in question by any writer. He visited Rome, and submitted to Pope Julius III his profession of Faith, and received the *pallium* from His Holiness.

His successor Mar Ebedjesus[1] went to Rome, assisted at the last session of the Council of Trent, and was, according to Giamil,[2] one of the most celebrated Patriarchs of the Catholic Chaldæans. He sent his profession of Faith to Pius IV. For nearly twelve years he ruled the destinies of the Eastern Church.

He was succeeded by Ahthalla Simon, about whom Mar Elia, the Chaldæan Archbishop of Amed, in a letter to Cardinal Carafa in 1580, says[3]:—" After the death of Ebedjesus, Mar Ahthalla Simon, an old man of holy ways, already Archbishop, was elected Patriarch. On account of the successive wars that were being waged in his country, and as he did not live for more than two years, he was not able to procure confirmation from the holy Apostolic See"; and Mar Elia says that he had been asked by this Patriarch to go to Rome and supplicate for the *pallium*. Besides, Le Quien[4] places him in the list of Catholic Patriarchs. Joseph Asseman also holds the same view. Hence the orthodoxy of Mar Simon is established.

On the death of Mar Simon in 1582, Simon Denha was elected Patriarch in the same year. As he was ruling the Church at the time of the Synod of Diamper, it is very necessary to examine his religious convictions. Pope Gregory XIII, who examined his profession of Faith, was satisfied with his orthodoxy, and gave him the *pallium*, confirming him as Patriarch. Le Quien[6] gives him a place among the Catholic Patriarchs, and asserts that, owing to Turkish persecution, he transferred his Patriarchal See to Urumiah in Persia. Asseman[7] also places

---

[1] Catholic Encyclopædia. Article ' Persia ', pp. 772-773.
[2] Giamil, Op. cit. pp. 63-68.
[3] Ibid. p. 93.
[4] Op. cit. t. 2, 1160-1161.
[5] Giamil. Op. cit. pp. 88-97.
[6] Op. cit. t. 2, 1161.
[7] Op. cit. t. 3, pp. 720-730.

him in the series of Catholic Patriarchs. Giamil,[1] basing himself on Vatican documents, asserts that Simon Denha was a Catholic. He died only in 1600. Hence we see that the Patriarch Mar Simon Denha who was governing the Church in 1599 was a Catholic, and yet the Portuguese had ordered the people to condemn, reject and anathematise him as a Nestorian heretic.

Let us make a few more observations on some of the decrees of this interesting Synod. The fourth decree[2] of the fifth session reveals one of the chief objects of the authors of the Synod, *viz.*, as far as possible to substitute the Latin Rite for the Syrian Rite of the St. Thomas Christians. "The Roman Mass to be translated into Syriac. Forasmuch as the Syrian Mass is *too long* for priests that have a mind to celebrate daily, the Synod doth grant license for the translating of the Roman Mass into Syriac, desiring the Rev. Father Roz s.j., to undertake the work………… The Synod desires that the bishops of these parts give license that *the priests* of this diocese having letters dimissory from their prelates, *that do not know how to say Mass in Latin, may be permitted to say the Syrian Mass in their Churches, or at least the Roman translated with all its ceremonies into Syriac.*"

The twenty-fifth decree[3] of the eighth session is interesting because it shows how the bishops of the St. Thomas Christians have been, without sufficient evidence, called Nestorians by the authors of the Synod. It runs thus:—" It is commonly said that they (the Bishops Mar Sapor and Mar Prodh) came into these parts and wrought miracles, and returned afterwards to Babylon, from whence they came, others affirming that they died in Coulan (Quilon), there being nothing writ of them that is authentic, neither does it appear that they were ever canonised by the Church, but on the contrary, *since they came from Babylon, there is just cause to suspect they might be heretics.*" The last part of this decree gives us, as it were, a key to solve the Nestorianism of the bishops of the Syrian Christians.

---

[1] Op. cit. pp. 93-97.
[2] Hough, vol. II, p. 591.
[3] Ibid. pages between 656 and 666.

The third decree[1] of the fifth session condemns a so-called Nestorian ceremony in the Mass. This is the wording of the ceremony:—"In the Syriac Missals of this episcopate, there is an impious and sacrilegious rite prescribed; the priest holding the parted half of the host in his right hand, dipped in blood as the host is, makes the sign of the cross with it on the other half of the host placed in the paten, which done, he bends the wet portion of the host with the nail of the thumb of his right hand under the false idea that the blood would thus penetrate the body and consequently mix the sacred body and blood. This opinion and ceremony is a spontaneous outcome of the Nestorian heresy and its sectaries who impiously assert that under the species of the bread only the body exists without the sacred blood, and under the species of wine only blood without the body." The Syrian Cathanars (priests) are forbidden to perform this ceremony by virtue of holy obedience and under penalty of excommunication incurred *ipso facto.* Here it must be noted that this "Nestorian" ceremony in the Mass, and many other observances of the ancient Syro-Chaldæan Rite condemned by the Synod as heretical, and forbidden to be kept up under pain of excommunication incurred *ipso facto,* are still to be found in the Taksas of the Catholic Syrians of Malabar as well as in those of the Catholics of Babylon, both printed at Rome with the approbation of the Holy See, and are even to this day observed by them. Is it not very plain, then, that it was, to say the least, merely inacquaintance on the part of the authors of the Synod with the ancient customs and ceremonies of the Chaldæan Rite, that classed these observances and these ceremonies as a spontaneous outcome of the Nestorian heresy. This, it seems to me, is the reason why His Holiness the Pope in prescribing the Taksas for these Churches, did not pay the least regard to the so-called emendations of the Synod.

Now, as to the statement of the Archbishop Menezes that the Sacrament of Confirmation did not exist in the Malabar Church, Father Simon, Renaudotius and the learned Asseman have in no uncertain terms maintained that Menezes and his

---

[1] Hough, vol. II, p. 666.

colleagues knew nothing about the matter, and add that the Sacrament of Confirmation in the East is included in that of Baptism. Asseman and Renaudotius have also proved from the use of the Holy Oil, the Sacrament of Extreme Unction in the East, and finally Asseman[1] has probed the question to the bottom and shown that matrimony and auricular confession existed as Sacraments in the Malabar Church.

Only once did the authors of the Synod try their hand at altering and adding certain portions to the Syriac Scriptures, and on that occasion they have invariably betrayed their unfitness for the task they took upon themselves. Hough[2] says:—"The Syrians did not merit the censures fulminated against them, for they were not responsible for the absence from their testament of important passages to be supplied, *viz.*, John viii, 3-11, the second Epistle of St. Peter, the second and third of St. John, the Epistle of Jude, and the Book of Revelations. These identical passages are not to be found in the Syriac copy of Widmanstadius, nor in some very old Greek MSS." Hence this attempt once again shows the great mistake which the authors of the Synod made, of ascribing everything that did not tally with the Latin Ritual and Ceremonies to the Nestorianism of the St. Thomas Christians.

We shall conclude these remarks on the Synod with the observations of Asseman as given by Mr. Mackenzie in the Travancore State Manual.[3] Asseman, in the course of answering the charges brought against the Synod, frankly admits that the Synod of Diamper made several mistakes; "first, in thinking that the passages wanting in the Syrian Bible had been wilfully omitted, whereas scholars afterwards saw that these gaps agree with gaps in some MSS. in Europe; second, in the matter and form of Holy Orders; third, in mistaking for the formala of baptism a proclamation that the child was baptised; fourth, in saying that Holy Oils were not used and Confirmation was unknown; fifth, in saying that Masses for the dead were unknown; sixth, in forbidding the eating of meat on

---

[1] Op. cit. t. 4, p. 318.
[2] Op. cit. vol. II, p. 532.
[3] Ibid. vol. II, p. 179.

Saturdays, and lastly, in making unnecessary changes in the Syrian Liturgy." Asseman attributes these mistakes on the part of the Portuguese clergy, who managed the Synod, to their ignorance of the Syrian Rite and of ancient Oriental Rites, to an excessive study of the Roman Ceremonial and a wish to wean these Christians from a Ritual which had been associated in the minds of the Portuguese with Nestorian errors.

It must, however, be admitted that some of the decrees of the Synod forbade actual Nestorian ceremonies or errors that had crept into this Church; for instance, some of the Taksas contained the names of Nestorius and his sectaries, and a few of the books, burned by Dom Menezes, were undoubtedly Nestorian books or contained Nestorian errors. Now how are these facts to be explained? The explanation is not to be sought; as we have seen, in maintaining that the Syrian Church as a whole was ever Nestorian. The untenableness of such a theory, I hope, I have sufficiently proved in these pages. The real explanation, and the one forced upon me by a special study of this period of the history of the Malabar Church, seems to be the following.

We have seen that in 1578 a Nestorian Bishop, Mar Simon, came to Malabar, remained in these parts for seven years, and that, on his deportation by the Portuguese, his Vicar-General Mar Jacob carried on the schism for twelve more years. The best authorities are, as we have said, agreed on these facts. Hence, during a period of nearly twenty years, Nestorian Taksas, Nestorian books, and with them Nestorian doctrines and ceremonies, speedily spread within the Syrian Church, especially as the tenth decree of the fifth session of the Synod testifies, the Syrian Bishops coming from Babylon were rather ignorant and careless. There was thus a small party of the St. Thomas Christians who had actually become Nestorians. It is very probable that these few Nestorian Syrian Christians were all present at the Synod, because after the Synod we do not even once hear mention made of Nestorians in Malabar. Moreover, their Vicar-General Jacob died in 1598, so that, at the time of the Synod, they were without a religious head.

There is, therefore, very great probability, that, left without a guide, they all accepted Catholicism at the Synod. Hence, wherever real Nestorian errors are pointed out in the decrees of the Synod, they are to be attributed to this small following of Nestorians among the St. Thomas Christians. That this can be the only valid explanation, is amply proved, I hope, from some of the sessions and decrees of the Synod which we have examined, and which indicate in the clearest terms that the Syrian Church in Malabar as a whole was ' Roman ' Catholic before the Synod of Diamper.